SMART GOVERNMENT:

Bureaucracy with a Business Brain

Commission for A New Georgia

Sharon McMahon

Mercer University Press
Macon GA
2010

MUP/SP100
ISBN 978-0-88146-229-6

© 2010 Mercer University Press
1400 Coleman Avenue
Macon, Georgia 31207

FIRST EDITION

Books published by Mercer University Press are printed on acid free paper that meets the requirements of American National Standard for Information Sciences—Permanence of Paper for Printed Library Materials.

Mercer University Press is a member of Green Press initiative (greenpressinitiative.org), a nonprofit organization working to help publishers and printers increase their use of recycled paper and decrease their use of fiber derived from endangered forests. This book is printed on recycled paper.

Library of Congress Cataloging-in-Publication Data
McMahon, Sharon, 1949-
  Smart government : bureaucracy with a business brain : Commission for a New
  Georgia / Sharon McMahon. – 1st ed.
     p. cm.
  Includes bibliographical references and index.
  ISBN 978-0-88146-229-6 (hardcover : alk. paper)
  1. Georgia. Commission for a New Georgia. 2. Public administration–Georgia.
  3. Georgia–Politics and government–1951- I. Title.
  JK4331.M36 2009
  351.758–dc22
  2010030106

GOVERNOR SONNY PERDUE

A Message to the People of Georgia

In 2002, I asked the people of Georgia for the great privilege and opportunity to serve as their Governor. I promised to restore confidence and trust in our government.

For eight years I've made it a top priority to deliver the highest return for our citizens' investment in government. We do that by managing for value — making sure our tax dollars get the best results for the greatest good at the lowest possible cost.

I believe that Georgians deserve to live in the Best-Managed State in America — a goal too important to be a government effort alone. So we forged a partnership with Georgia's top executives who lead highly successful enterprises in the business world. We asked them to bring their best ideas to the challenge of making our government a 21st Century model of smart management.

The Commission for A New Georgia and its task forces of top-flight professionals have been our real-world consultants. They volunteered their time and generated a wealth of recommendations to achieve efficiency and cost-effectiveness in the way we do business. We acted on their advice and held ourselves accountable for results.

Today, Georgia ranks among the top five states in management performance. The challenge now is to sustain our gains and make it the new standard for business-as-usual in a best-managed state.

On behalf of the people of Georgia, I offer my tremendous appreciation to the Commission members and hundreds of citizens who served on our task forces for impeccable service to their state.

Sonny Perdue

SONNY PERDUE, GOVERNOR OF GEORGIA

CONTENTS

IT'S NOT FOR COFFEE TABLES

From the first press release in May 2003 announcing Governor Sonny Perdue's business-led Commission for A New Georgia, co-chairs Joe Rogers and Bob Hatcher have made a point of declaring that "We're not in this to produce a coffee-table book."

A book showed up anyway – less to sit on a coffee-table, more to sit by a coffee cup. It wraps its pages around the story of how smart people from the worlds of business and bureaucracy put their heads together to make Georgia one of the best-managed states in America.

America understands better today than seven years ago what "best-managed" means: smaller, smarter, more sustainable government, right-sized to its resources and getting the job done with the leanest possible management.

The massive machinery of government isn't wired to reset its workings, just because circumstances suddenly turn dire. Re-engineering the enterprise is a rigorous 360-degree process from the top down, from the bottom up and crossways… simultaneously.

For seven years, the Commission for A New Georgia (CNG) has served as the catalyst for re-engineering Georgia's government to be not only smaller, smarter and leaner, but also faster, friendlier and easier for citizens. The transformation has worked its way through government with surprising momentum.

PUBLISHING THIS BOOK SERVES TWO PURPOSES. The first is to deliver a strong message from some of Georgia's most respected corporate executives: Managing for sustainable government must stay a focal point of effective governing, no matter who is Governor.

The second purpose is to demonstrate that the Commission is a model that gets results and generates solutions for sustainability. CNG's strategies for success were not spontaneous or sporadic. They were systematic and sustained. They started with the architecture of the stand-alone Commission structure, the work plan for a continuing series of task forces and the guarantee of accountability in high offices for implementing change. The process is integral to the end result.

Governor Sonny Perdue was emphatic that he did not want a book about himself or a self-serving opus on his eight-year governorship. He insisted the focus stay on the Commission for A New Georgia. Nevertheless, the account cannot be told apart from the state's Chief Executive, whose ideas and iron will waged the quiet revolution that led Georgia to the top tier of America's best-managed states. Leadership matters.

In a series of interviews, Governor Perdue spoke in depth about critical elements in his strategy for management reform. More professorial than political, excerpts speak to the Governor's desire to restore trust in government and "add value for citizens by managing well."

FOR THE RECORD, no CNG board or task force member was paid by the Commission or the state. These citizens worked without portfolio or blue-ribbon status. Extraordinarily busy executives took seriously the mission of modernizing operations in government that their own businesses had changed 20 years ago.

More than 30 individuals who contributed to the Commission's work were interviewed or shared their insights to shape this report. But hundreds more people worked together to create the body of work it represents. They include

Governor's staff, CNG members, accomplished citizens who served on task forces, partners in top-notch international consulting firms, legislators, agency leaders and state employees. The Commission was originally chartered for a two-year partnership. Still active when the Governor won a second term, Commission board members were offered the choice to bow out after a job well done. Their unanimous response was to stay the course as long as there was work to do.

IN 2008, WASHINGTON POST COLUMNIST DAVID BRODER covered the announcement of the Pew Trust's triennial "Best Managed States" report card. Georgia was the "most improved" state that year, and Governor Perdue was invited by the Pew Center on the States and *Governing* magazine to talk about his experience in managing for performance. Broder made this observation:

> The drama of this Presidential campaign obscures the fact that for most of us, the government services that most directly affect our lives are delivered from state capitols or city halls.

> A new generation of governors is focusing on management, in part because citizens are so skeptical of government, but also because tough economic times demand it and because their own backgrounds point them in that direction.

> As Governor Perdue said, managing government is 'not a sexy issue.' But after 17 or 18 presidential candidates offer rhetorical salve for the widespread distrust of government, it was refreshing to learn what some practitioners are actually doing to improve its performance.

THE LESSONS LEARNED through Georgia's seven-year, public-private partnership are both fundamental and forward-looking. They are here to be passed to others who believe that better government is forever a work in progress.

UNDER NEW MANAGEMENT: GEORGIA'S PUBLIC ENTERPRISE

"A new generation of governors is focusing on management, in part because citizens are so skeptical of government, but also because tough economic times demand it and because their own backgrounds point them in that direction."

DAVID BRODER, WASHINGTON POST, MARCH 2008

Timing is an idea whose leader has come.

Georgia's 2002 gubernatorial election overthrew more than a century of political history. Behind those headlines, another revolution was stirring. The election of Sonny Perdue brought together the personal chemistry and political conditions right to depose the past-century regime of bureaucratic business-as-usual and establish a 21st Century model of smart, sustainable government for Georgia.

Not every leader has charisma, but all have chemistry – inborn determinants of how they think, act and lead. The new Administration manifested the analytic DNA of the Governor, a methodical thinker who locks on data, trend-lines, outcomes and metrics and who acts on hard evidence. "I'm not particularly intuitive in decision-making," Perdue has said. "I need facts." Agency heads quickly got the gist as budget hearings turned from annual pitches for more money to an audit of program priorities, performance and projections.

Perdue's dual careers as a self-made business owner and a six-term state senator shared his left-brain penchant for management science, which he equates with the general idea of "engineering to make things run better." Although he never took a career profile assessment, Perdue is sure it would have pointed to a bent for industrial engineering. "I'm a process, efficiency, effectiveness type of guy. I just want things to work. That's what drives me."

As Perdue operated in parallel worlds of business and government, he contrasted the rigor of management practices and standards in the private and public sectors. In his analysis, the state's massive bureaucracy was woefully un-managed, but not un-manageable. He took the job as Chief Executive Officer of the State of Georgia with the firm notion that the CEO's role is to manage the business of government. This linked to another marker of his make-up: a stubborn intentionality to get done whatever job he took on.

As for political conditions, the new leader was preparing to govern a world wobbling on its axis. The election of a Republican governor brought the first turnover in party control at the Capitol since the 1870s. Suddenly, a long-shot candidate ignored by the power structure rode a silent swell of small-dollar donors to victory. It shocked the pollsters as much as the fatly-financed incumbent. Perdue relished the ability to walk into the office clear of political debts and free of entanglements with the established regime – free to move about outside the box. In fact, the box had been blown up.

"I literally had no obligations, financial or otherwise, other than to the people and their expectation that I would do my best to make Georgia the best it could be," Perdue said. "That gave me great liberty to make decisions."

Overarching the politics of the day was the lingering fiscal pall of the 9/11 recession, Georgia's then-worst economic crisis since the Great Depression. In 2002, the budget had bled a billion dollars in revenue losses, with deficits mounting as Perdue took office.

The morning after the election, the incoming leader confronted the economic imperative for decisive action, as well as a historic opportunity to set a new agenda for governing.

A QUIET REVOLUTION – DRAMATIC CHANGE MINUS THE DRAMA

"When the people hand you the keys to the Office of Governor, it is an awesome stewardship responsibility. I don't own it. It belongs to the people of Georgia. I've been allowed to manage it for the time being. It is my role and goal as a steward to hand the keys back, eight years later, leaving the state better than I found it."

GOVERNOR SONNY PERDUE

Candidate Perdue had run on a platform of restoring trust in government by managing its resources and services responsibly and responsively. Basic to his definition of effective stewardship was delivering on value – in the vernacular, more bang for the taxpayers' buck.

Perdue disdained what he considered "flashy, headline-grabbing programs" and "grandiose" projects with a starting bid of a billion dollars. His signature agenda would be the contrary: a methodical, disciplined plan for management reform. Once underway, it would bring transformative management tools, best business practices, smart technologies and an aggressive implementation strategy to the task. The order of business was to shape up the state enterprise, putting its functions in top running order and fixing broken systems that leak money and don't work well for citizens.

Efficiencies and financial systems have the potential to generate substantial savings and recovered revenue. But it isn't just about money. Good management is about value. Efficient, effective, economical government is the bedrock of fiscal resilience as the population inevitably grows and revenues inevitably wax and wane.

From the Governor's CEO perspective, a sound operational infrastructure which functions at peak performance is fundamental to effective governing and essential to the success of all of its undertakings.

His announced goal was "to make Georgia the best-managed state in America."

Not exactly a slogan to light up a marquee.

Perdue and his advisory team set about recalibrating the measures of value in a sustainable public enterprise. The parameters were straightforward: smaller, smarter government; more bang for the tax buck; faster, friendlier, easier customer service.

To reach a better situation, Perdue knew the transformation of government must evolve holistically in a deliberate and organized way which involves people, processes and performance measures.

The larger, longer view he had in mind was transformation of the culture of government to be principle-led, customer-centered, results-oriented and data-driven.

"Georgia was in dire need of a transformation," Perdue said. "This doesn't just happen with sweeping legislation or by executive order. It happens slowly, a result of individuals making a difference… in a staff meeting, in a cubicle, on the phone. It happens in the daily decisions made, not just by agency heads, but by employees. It happens when you give people the resources they need to be efficient."

THE GOVERNOR'S CHALLENGE STARTED AT MACRO-ALTITUDE, classifying the parts of government and pulling them together into a coherent enterprise.

A new governance template was needed to position management at a level that would have tangible impact on improving performance.

The first piece would be a corporate-style executive structure with reporting and communication lines designed to bring agencies out of their silos and into the business of the state.

A sensible, systematic process would be developed to isolate and analyze internal government functions that should be operated on an enterprise level. Customer service and leadership development initiatives would be directed at infusing the culture of government with a sense of public service and stewardship.

This was nothing less than a complete overhaul of the inner workings of government, beginning with a daunting list of pre-conditions to establish:

- Understanding the state as an enterprise – how all its parts should work together coherently, eliminating redundancy and establishing clear lines of responsibility and authority.

- Right-sizing the essential responsibilities of government to its resources.

- Engineering lean, cost-efficient operations to deliver needed services.

- Tracking where the state spends its money and measuring the outcomes.

- Accurately accounting for the state's assets and their lifecycle costs.

- Shedding things government owns but doesn't use.

- High business standards and astute practices for managing finances.

- Program planning and budgeting based on defined objectives that enable the enterprise to serve the needs of its customers.

All were commonsensical tenets, but radical in their departure from the existing environment.

The tone of the transformation started deliberately low-key and stayed at that volume. Eventually someone, now anonymous, was inspired to describe what was happening inside Georgia's government as "a quiet revolution" – dramatic change without the drama.

WHERE IS THIS BOOK GOING?

"Georgia, under Perdue, has been one of the leaders in the push to make governments run better by importing and adapting management techniques, information systems and performance measures from the business world."
TRUST MAGAZINE, PEW CHARITABLE TRUST, OCTOBER 2008.

The preceding background has passed through the philosophy, ideas and personal characteristics of the key figure who took responsibility for driving the transformation of government – not just for a first term, or through a Commission stint – but continuously for eight years. Although "unique" is a descriptor applied advisedly, Governor Sonny Perdue appears a unique fit for the leadership qualities required to pull off a substantive, sustained management turnaround.

The political and economic dynamics have been touched upon to convey a sense of the times as a crucible for change.

This preface makes way for the story to move on to what actually changed and how it happened during the eight-year Perdue administration. It segues to the pivotal role of the Commission for A New Georgia and the hundreds of citizens who came forward to make government work better.

The story focuses on strategies, actions and the forces at play in the government arena. It follows the formation of the public/private initiative, taking a more or less chronological path to plot the design and development from point to point.

KEEPING THE END IN MIND

Endeavors this big don't just spring full-blown like Athena from the forehead of Zeus. They build from a situation that inspires a vision and are moved forward by ideas, dedicated people and a plan that works.

Here's a preview of what happened from 2003 to 2010:

The Governor's aspiration for Georgia to become America's Best-Managed State rallied the troops up and down the line with surprising force and focus. In 2008, Georgia earned one of the five top scores in the Government Performance evaluation by the Pew Center on the States. Georgia was the "most improved" state, making a giant leap from its mediocre grade on the 2005 GPP report card.

Commission for A New Georgia co-chairs Bob Hatcher and Joe Rogers were awarded the National Governor's Association 2010 Distinguished Service Award to State Government, recognizing their leadership of the Commission's work.

Billions of dollars of previously unaccounted-for state assets – buildings, vehicles and aircraft, equipment, purchases, bank holdings – are now fully documented in comprehensive enterprise-wide databases and managed for maximum lifecycle value.

Rapid process improvement, lean management, new technologies and professional leadership in agencies are bringing government operations up to speed with 21st Century business standards. In major operational areas, particularly customer service and procurement, Georgia is nationally recognized as a leading innovator of best practices.

The efficiency and accountability imposed by implementation of CNG recommendations have generated more than a billion dollars in value through cost savings and containment, recovered revenues and sale of surplus property.

The business mindset modeled by Commission initiatives has permeated the workings of government beyond task force areas, spreading the "best practice" bug systemically, office by office, day by day. This is what culture change in government looks like.

By HAPPENSTANCE OF HISTORY, Perdue's eight-year administration was book-ended by the recessions of 9/11 and the credit collapse. While governors don't control wars or Wall Street, they do manage governments that impact millions of people and cost billions of dollars. Perdue believed management is a powerful tool of governing that must be utilized to maximize value and make state government more resourceful, responsive and resilient. He also saw the private sector as a powerful partner in retooling management of the public enterprise.

When the Big Bottom fell out in 2008, Georgia was years along in imple-menting managerial practices recommended by national experts like the Pew Center on the States. In contrast to the 2002 recession, Georgia managed the Great Recession better in worse conditions, the Governor told the 2009 *Governing* Conference on Managing for Performance.

"This time," Perdue said, "because of the culture, the attitude and the workmanlike competence, it's been better. I won't say easier, but better. Had we not put in place the management changes we have over the past five or six years, we would just be adrift out here.

"The current recession is much worse than in 2003, but it's been handled experientially better: from a confidence of management to leaders, not just presenting their budget but knowing it inside and out. They know what they're spending their money on, and they know what their people are doing. They understand the best utilization of resources must be applied. That mentality is contagious. When just a few leaders get the celebration for that, more and more start to do the same."

"In 2003, when Governor Sonny Perdue set up his Commission for A New Georgia, it sounded like a recipe for one more unread manifesto doomed to gather more dust than interest. But the Governor meant business. And since its creation, the Commission has been slowly, quietly and deliberately infiltrating Georgia state government with best practices from private industry."

GOVERNING

MARCH 2008

PAST AS PREP: LESSONS OF A LESSER RECESSION

Chapter One encounters the state of the State after the 2002 election, a government midstream in recession and mid-year in a budget projected to be a half-billion dollars short. Agency heads, their budget defenses in hand, faced a new Governor-elect – and began to understand that business as they knew it had just been turned on its head.

YOU CAN'T IMMEDIATELY PREPARE FOR A CRISIS
. . . .
NEVER MIND THE CHEESE, WHERE'S OUR STUFF?
. . . .
THE MINDSET OF MORE MEETS THE REALITY OF LESS
. . . .
WHEN THE RAINS COME...
. . . .
GETTING THE RIGHT PEOPLE ON THE BUS
. . . .
GOVERNMENT IS THE PEOPLE'S BUSINESS
. . . .
WHY MANAGEMENT MATTERS

"You can't immediately prepare for a crisis."

SONNY PERDUE, GOVERNOR OF GEORGIA

On November 4, 2002, Georgians elected the state's first Republican governor since a New York-born Reconstructionist literally fled from the office 131 years before. The election night shocker pulled off by Sonny Perdue caught incumbent Roy Barnes flatfooted, while the Capitol turned a historic flip in party power. Politics were popping all over the place.

The fireworks in the Gold Dome flared against the black clouds of the worst economy since the Great Depression. Remember the times: Georgia's key industries – airlines, construction, auto plants, tourism – were battered by the economic shockwaves of September 11, 2001. Unemployment rolls swelled by 30,000. Eighteen months of revenue downturns put the state in a $620 million hole. Perdue learned after the election that the actual shortfall for the mid-year budget was worse than admitted by the previous Administration. Despite the five percent across-the-board slash by the 2002 General Assembly in passing the Fiscal Year 2003 budget, a second round of "hold-backs" would be required of agencies by January 1, 2003.

The Governor-elect had less than 30 days after the election to deconstruct and rebuild the current and coming years' budgets by his standards. Allocation reviews were already far along in the decision process. Within days of the election, Perdue and his temporary executive staff set up transition operations in borrowed offices in a downtown building. He commenced budget hearings the same week. For the next month, he spent 150 mind-grinding hours in sessions with department heads and analysts, figuring how to slice and dice $459 million in mid-year spending deferrals.

The Perdue transition team and the sitting agency heads were at the same time piecing together the budget for Fiscal Year 2004. The proposed appropriations would factor in continued reductions, plus a one-percent austerity cut. Even with that, filling the hole in the adjusted FY03 and coming FY04 budgets required siphoning more than $280 million from the state's "rainy day" reservoir. The withdrawal left the state's reserves at $50 million, equated by one analyst to "shelf dust" or a "rounding error" compared to a budget of $16.5 billion.

NEVERMIND THE CHEESE, WHERE'S OUR STUFF?

"Let's ask everyone who has a state vehicle to drive to Braves Stadium… and count these things."

JOHN WATSON, PERDUE TRANSITION VICE CHAIR

The hearings pried the lids off a mess of canned worms. One was government cars.

The easy cuts were made in the Legislature's first pass at skimming the FY03 budget. By the mid-year round of holdbacks, the process was digging deeper. Perdue wanted to examine inventories of state-owned assets such as vehicles, real estate and various kinds of assigned equipment.

That was a problem. There weren't any statewide record systems – just individual entries in various accounts siloed in more than 100 agencies, commissions and authorities. Not only were there no central inventories of hard counts, but expenses associated with cost of ownership of state possessions were undecipherable in the hodgepodge of different record-keeping methods within agencies and departments.

In particular, state vehicles wore a bulls-eye. Anecdotally, taxpayers griped about Crown Vics with government tags parked in driveways of state employees who commuted to work courtesy of the state's fuel card. Or office staff seen piling out of a state-marked car for lunch at a nice restaurant. Nobody in government could factually say how much it was costing the state to own and operate its stables of vehicles. Who got the use of personally-assigned wheels? How many cars, pick-ups and vans did the agencies buy each year, and with what justification? What was the state's bill for servicing, insuring, and fueling the fleet, disposing of junkers or totaling wrecked vehicles? Unknown.

One fact was known: Georgia, the ninth largest state, had the second largest state-owned fleet in the nation – by best guess, approximately one passenger-carrying vehicle for every five state employees.

"In the transition, we had this open joke… let's ask everyone who has a state vehicle to drive to Braves Stadium and see if we can actually count these things," said transition vice chair John Watson, who later served as chief of staff in Perdue's first term. "We didn't know, and there was no data.

"I remember trying to get inventories of everything the state owned. We went through the same process with a number of other issues, like cell phones," Watson said. "We had to wonder, 'How do we measure what we own from standpoints of quality, fraud and cost?' Traditionally, no one had cared about that."

THE UNACCOUNTED PROLIFERATION of state vehicles wasn't the biggest problem facing state management – not even close. Cars were just a common, simple-to-see example of how assets were accumulated but not accounted for in their lifetime as state property.

Multiply the unknowns by truly massive state operations, such as the annual investment in an estimated 15,000 state-owned buildings, plus 1,700 leases for rental space. State government was the largest property holder in Georgia, but had no central register of deeds or leases. No records were accessible to assess conditions of structures, maintenance and utility costs, square footage in use, vacancy rates and idle land – the statistical stuff of basic property management and stewardship.

The smaller stuff of government also added up. Every year agencies purchase several billion dollars worth of equipment, supplies and services – from stacks of sticky notes to laptop computers to janitorial contracts and thousands of other things. Most purchasing was piecemeal, under the radar of procurement practices. Agencies were paying way too many different prices – sometimes double – for the same common items. Purchasing was so random that a state procurement agent said if anyone wanted to determine how many laptops or cell phones were bought in a given year, it was faster and more accurate to ask vendors for state sales receipts than to seek the information from agency records.

After 11 years serving in the State Senate, the new Governor was not blind to the many ways tax dollars travel from the citizen's wallet to an invoice for a state sedan or an earmark for someone's pet project. "Every year, I saw millions of tax dollars streaming into operations, services, assets and programs in a hundred agencies and authorities, with implicit budget autonomy. I saw allocations decided by power politics, personal affinity and leaps of faith – hardly ever by data and analysis. In practice, bureaucracy ran itself, and we paid the bills."

That's how budgets keep growing as more money keeps rolling in. In 2002 the revenue began rolling backwards.

FROM THE GOVERNOR'S NOTEPAD...
Get accurate records for state assets; cost-of-ownership data.

THE MINDSET OF MORE MEETS THE REALITY OF LESS

"The culture of that time was all input-driven. It was all about needing more resources, needing more everything. There was no culture of accountability for outcomes whatsoever. That was a foreign concept."

GOVERNOR SONNY PERDUE

The transition team's weeks of recessionary budget hearings served as learning opportunities in many ways. They put Perdue eye-to-eye with agency leaders who would soon report to him. It provided an interview setting in which to probe commissioners' understanding of the efficacy of expenditures in achieving the objectives of their mission – in short what was their bang for the buck? Performance outcomes were not in the vocabulary of budget requests.

"We were facing a culture in the state which had never seen revenues go down consecutive years except two times in history. Once was in the Great Depression. This was the second," Perdue explained. "Agency heads were not ever used to having less than they had the year before. So we weren't dealing with leaders in our agencies who managed with that in mind. It was purely a culture of inputs – expecting what they had last year, plus inflation, plus annualization, plus enhancements.

"So that's what we had to reverse, coming with a new face and a lack of preparation."

Perdue, the business owner, was dismayed to discover that many agency chiefs were wholly delegating budget matters to their financial people and "didn't know what was in their checkbooks." In fact they often didn't know what was in their agency budget requests. In the CEO's estimation, "A company's checkbook should tell you what's important to them."

Perdue came to office already sold on the concept of program-based budgeting. The P-BB approach was based on evaluating requests for funding agency programs by priority of state need and measures of desired outcomes.

"In that first budget cycle, I just had a very simple mindset free of budgets, revenues or expenditures. We had every agency go through the basic question: Why are you here? Tell us what it is you do and why we can't live without it. Each agency needed to justify their purpose for being there and getting a share of our investors' money."

Perdue said the hearings handed him a "tactic of change" to refocus managers from inputs to outcomes.

> "At that time, the state budgeted by line items in object classes – for example, travel, personnel, telecomm, contract fees per diem and so on. Those broad classes said nothing about what we were doing with the money.
>
> "The first tactic we used was to make the agencies break out all the programs they had and prioritize them, from the most important – what can't we do without – to what we should do and then what is just nice to have. We allowed time for leaders to articulate why they chose what they did and then allocated the money based on the value delivered by those programs.
>
> "This was program-based budgeting. It was an evolutionary work in progress that is going on to this day."

Some leaders adapted quickly to P-BB; others not so much. "There was some hide and seek early on, and I think a few people felt they could conduct business-as-usual," said Perdue. "But I dove into the process because I wanted to know it, and I wanted others to know it. We continually had to assess who could operate in the metrics of accountability and who could not."

Perdue compares agency angst over the budget conversion to college faculty who fretted over the quarter system converting to semesters. "You find those professors who used the same lessons for 20 years, and their biggest complaint is, 'I'm going to have to change my notes.'

"You learn through questioning, and that was one of the ways we determined the leaders that probably needed to find another career – and those who were doing a good job and wanted to do even better."

The budget process, Watson said, became the Governor's litmus test for those managers "able to successfully have measurable results with good outcomes for the taxpayer."

Celeste Osborne, deputy chief of finance from 2003 to 2009, was an able administrator who served in top levels of state finance through five governors. As a participant in hundreds of budget reviews, she clearly saw a substantive difference in budget development before and after P-BB:

> "For the first time, the Governor has been able to say, 'What is the return on investment for the state of Georgia and to the public on this program?' That has been a defining initiative of really looking into what it costs to run programs, in lieu of just looking at gross dollars and personal services, contracts and so on, which have been the focus in the past."

IN HIS FIRST BUDGET MESSAGE to the General Assembly as Governor, Perdue laid out the strategy for a value-building process for sustainable government, seeing a silver lining in the lesson of recession:

> "We can and should see this as an opportunity to improve our overall fitness by reforming the budget process. We have four years to do so. We must return to an era of true results-based, performance-based budgeting. Every year we will examine each agency or department's funding request in its entirety. Line items that are no longer needed or that do not align with our core principles will be eliminated. And we will carry out a sustained series of performance audits to ensure that Georgians are getting the best value for their tax dollars."

He added a warning that would be reprised sooner than anyone feared to imagine: "We must resist any temptation to mortgage our future, and our children's future, to deal with the challenges on our watch."

FROM THE GOVERNOR'S NOTEPAD...
Reform budget process to prioritize programs, define objectives, show outcome data.

WHEN THE RAINS COME...

"The surpluses we enjoyed in recent years aren't there anymore. Decisions we deferred until another day... that day has come."
GOVERNOR SONNY PERDUE, 2003 BUDGET MESSAGE

Another red flag that shot up the pole was the disposition of surpluses – those bonus funds in the coffer in the years when revenue collections exceed the budget. The Governor was bothered by previous administrations' impulses to spend the mid-year surplus as fast as possible and institutionalize the expenditure as an ongoing appropriation. His particular peeve was the homestead exemption, passed with surplus funding in 1999 and legislated to continue as long as there was a mid-year bump in revenue. Meanwhile, the state's savings account was left insufficiently funded for any significant exigency, as revealed by the rapid depletion of the reserve.

"This added fuel to the fire for the Governor to improve not only management of operations, but the financial side as well," according to Trey Childress, a member of the transition team and later the director of the Governor's Office of Planning and Budget.

After the dangerously low drawdown of the rainy day fund, the Governor took specific measures to build back reserves, Childress said. From the beginning of his term, Perdue always played revenue projections on the conservative side to leave a margin for savings, and he proposed legislation to exceed the cap on reserves. This was coupled with "aggressive efforts to bend down the trend-line on explosive areas like Medicaid, below double-digit growth."

In Childress' assessment, "If this hadn't been done, we wouldn't have had the means to bank away money in our rainy day fund and wouldn't have had the flexibility of a $1.6 billion reserve in 2008 when things really fell off the cliff.

"I cannot even imagine what we would have done in this far worse recession if we were still seeing some of the patterns when we started in 2003."

FROM THE GOVERNOR'S NOTEPAD...
Build future surpluses into the plan for sustainable government.

GETTING THE RIGHT PEOPLE ON THE BUS

"We had people who had been leading agencies in state government for years and had never been in the same room."

GOVERNOR SONNY PERDUE

Other priorities besides budget were occupying the transition team. Appointments were being vetted for key administration positions, and this is where the Governor's idea for a new executive structure began to take shape.

The way it had always been done by past governors was to have the chief of staff serve as the "bureaucracy czar" over all direct reports. In Georgia, that numbered about 85 heads of agencies plus more than a dozen attached authorities and commissions. The totality of responsibility comprised nearly 100,000 employees and about 2,000 programs serving 9.5 million citizens.

Perdue flatly states, "I don't care how good you are, no one person can deal with 85 direct reports."

The Governor's Chief of Staff throughout his first year in office was Eric Tanenblatt, who served as one of the volunteer leaders of the transition until Perdue appointed him to head the executive staff.

"Early on we realized government needed to do a better job delivering services to citizens," Tanenblatt said. "In talking to former governors of Georgia and their senior staff, we learned that governors didn't interact much with agency heads unless there was a problem."

Perdue soon realized, "We had people who had been leading organizations and agencies in state government for years, in similar areas, who had never been in the same room with one another.

"There was no synergy, because they felt they operated independently and didn't know or care what another agency was doing, as long as they didn't infringe on what they believed to be their business."

There was a natural fall line between agencies with core missions to deliver public services and agencies that focus on internal government functions, which are primarily revenue-driven. Perdue divided the agencies by external/internal responsibilities and drew reporting lines respectively to two newly established positions of Chief Operating Officer and Chief Financial Officer. The Chief of Staff became the infielder, handling the management of the Governor's Office, including policy, communications and scheduling.

The offices of State COO and State CFO significantly revamped the executive structure and its relationship to the bureaucratic administrators. With the three "chiefs," Perdue had a total of six direct reports, who also included the executive counsel, the inspector general and the director of homeland security. There had been serious talk of creating a Chief Administrative Officer over the enterprise functions of property management, technology services, procurement and human resources. The Governor balked at the appearance of "too many chiefs" making six-figure salaries in his office. He felt the COO and CFO could manage the full range of state business within their given realms, as well as allow for needed direct interaction between key agency heads and the Governor.

THE REDEFINED, CORPORATE-STYLE ORGANIZATION CHART was intended to transform the dynamics at the top of the executive branch from political to managerial governance. It signaled an agenda of new business at many levels of meaning. In workaday practice, the new reporting arrangement created a platform for the agency leaders to have regular access to the top levels of executive authority, to interact among their colleagues in other agencies and to relate to the larger, common enterprise they served. This was a whole new culture for state leadership.

Perdue revealed his organizational plans to state business leaders in December 2002 at the Georgia Economic Outlook Conference. He made a point of describing his concept for using "models from the business world" to improve accountability and efficient use of resources.

"With 100,000 employees and more than 80 departments reporting to the Governor, managing state government is like trying to hug an octopus," Perdue told the business group. "To improve accountability, we're adopting a management model similar to what many of you use in your own companies."

This was also the first public announcement of the new CFO and COO positions to coordinate finance and service missions. "The lines of responsibility will be clear, and we'll have every hand in every agency pulling together in the same direction to better serve the human needs of Georgia."

To fill pivotal positions of the new chiefs for operating and finance, the Governor reached out to seasoned, successful executives from large business-sector institutions. They understood from experience how the distinct roles of divisions work in concert for the success of the greater enterprise. The state's first Chief Operating Officer, named in January 2003, was Jim Lientz, retired President of Bank of America's MidSouth Division and a highly respected Atlanta business leader. The interim role of transition budget director, precursor to the CFO appointment, had been filled by University of Georgia Senior Vice President of Finance and Administration Hank Huckaby. His long leadership as the state's planning and budget director made him the most knowledgeable finance insider in government. He shepherded the Administration through the perils of their first legislative session. Six months later, the new Chief Financial Officer was on board in the person of Tommy Hills, who had served as Wachovia's Executive Vice President and Atlanta City President.

Coming into government, Lientz was stunned to discover that the state's top administrators rarely spoke and almost never collaborated on state business.

"I was surprised the individual leaders of these agencies didn't work together on a regular basis. I was surprised that teamwork wasn't emphasized more, and surprised there wasn't more communication," he said.

"But what we've found is that people want that. They want to work together and be held accountable. Any organization has their share of lone wolves, and that just doesn't work. But most people want to be part of the team."

The schedule of weekly chiefs' meetings created a communication interchange for regular dialogue about the business of the state. A big advantage of the increased vertical and horizontal communication was development of pipelines to surface accurate, firsthand information that was customarily siloed with no outlet for sharing.

"The process of creating and giving status to a business-like organization is ultimately the Governor's way of trying to structure things to create accurate information and good decisions," said John Watson, who succeeded

Tanenblatt as Chief of Staff in 2004. "At a strategic level the Governor has a curious mind, a real appropriate fascination with data and the belief that good information is necessary to drive decisions, whether public policy or business. Without a foundation of factual information and data, you are left with the inability as an executive to make quality decisions."

Watson said Perdue's insistence on accurate, detailed data to back-up reported information provoked some negative reactions in administrators who were used to a culture where face value was accepted practice.

> "What had traditionally been the perspective of the state's CEO was to presume a level of accuracy in the information being provided by the bureaucracy. I believe that was because running the business of government had been a second-tier priority to the legislative component of governing.
>
> "This Governor's unique background as a successful entrepreneur led him to ask questions and require data-driven facts that really challenged state agencies in a manner they weren't used to or prepared for."

FOR AGENCY LEADERS WONDERING if the detail-pickiness would be a passing post-election fad, the epiphany came at the Governor-elect's first breakfast meeting with 80-plus agency and department heads.

Perdue gave an inspirational speech which concluded by dropping a bomb-shell. All agency heads were to tender their resignations – effective immediately. The Governor said he needed "the liberty of a clean start" as he pursued his agenda for a New Georgia.

Requesting resignations en masse is not unheard of in transitions, but the message was clear to present company: Perdue meant business about changing business-as-usual. He invited agency heads who wanted to continue to serve to submit a resume and go though a re-interviewing process. "I don't care whether you have an R or a D behind your name," the Governor assured the administrators. "I am looking for talented people to serve Georgia."

More than a dozen commissioners were formally back on board shortly after the inauguration. For the majority, resignations remained in the drawer if needed.

"There was a period of time we had to go through a triage of understanding if a person was capable of being brought to our way of thinking and giving them the opportunity to jump on the bus," Watson said. "Were there some people who wanted to get on the bus from day one? Absolutely. There are a lot of great people in government who were refreshed by an environment that was intellectually challenging and took their issues seriously."

The spotlight of executive-level attention caused some squirming at first. "The culture then was not to be on the radar enough to be noticed by the Governor, because nine times out of 10 it would be for a bad reason," Watson said. "I think the COO/CFO organizational model was helpful as a mechanism of communication for interaction rather than disciplinary measures."

The change in communication with agency managers from punitive to positive also turned the spotlight on up-and-coming innovators who wanted the chance to shine and were willing to take on challenges and risks, trusting they would have support at the top. This would become a driving factor for successful change initiatives, including the reorganization of drivers' services, the privatization of enterprise technology and communications systems, and rapid process improvement transformations led by customer service teams.

FROM THE GOVERNOR'S NOTEPAD...

Make leadership development a priority to build a culture of engagement.

GOVERNMENT IS THE PEOPLE'S BUSINESS

"Many of us Republicans campaign on promises to run government like a business. I might have thought that in my Senate career, but the fact is government is not a business and doesn't have the same motivations of profit. However, it does have return on investment for its investors – being the citizens – through value translation."

GOVERNOR SONNY PERDUE

Purists in worlds of private business and public administration might argue that "business" and "bureaucracy" are organizational opposites. One is run for profit, the other for the public welfare. One is management savvy and streamlined, the other senselessly snarled in red tape. One has accountability only to self-interested investors, and the other doesn't know the meaning of accountability.

Two realities of government coexist: its bureaucratic organization and its business operations. Its business is to provide the infrastructure and services which create conditions essential for living and working in the state. Its business is financed by investors, who are also its citizens and customers. The test is whether the public enterprise can be managed as a business-like organization to deliver the best value for the investment and the general welfare.

COO Jim Lientz, who has worked at the top levels of both the corporate and government worlds, readily recognized parallels that run through both.

"Government is an extremely large organization which has many characteristics of other large business organizations. It is not necessarily a business, but the dynamics and characteristics were what we, from the private sector, recognized.

"A lot of people in government don't see that as true, and they said business disciplines can't be applied. Nothing could be further from the truth. They hadn't thought about government as an enterprise which could be managed and led.

"Characteristic of large businesses, state government was not as accountable as it should have been and was not emphasizing basic tenets of communication, teamwork and return on investment. This is Business 101, but was foreign in the culture of government. It takes a fair amount of time to embed these principles in a culture, and it takes a leader who is dedicated and persistent."

THE CONCEPT THAT PULLS TOGETHER the organization and operations is the "enterprise" managing the totality of its resources to give maximum value for the tax dollar.

"We have to understand the role of services that the public enterprise is compelled to perform, but not profit from," Perdue acknowledges. "But there is no reason not to do these efficiently and effectively. It doesn't have a monetary return, but it gives value in many different ways, and our citizens are beneficiaries."

In the ideal world, a public enterprise is driven by the value motive, the optimum nexus of quality and cost in things that matter to the taxpayer. Applied to the business of government, value is counted in many ways – saving millions of dollars on the cost of government goods and services through smart purchasing, slashing turnaround time on state processes for transacting public business, accountability for a sound, safe infrastructure and customer-focused services.

Bureaucracies, though, are built to run on a stable funding source with a monopoly on services, which pretty much kills the motive to surpass the status quo in improving value. Their shops don't go out of business if they under-perform or deal customers shabby treatment and shoddy service. Successful businesses survive and thrive in a culture of innovation and improvement to increase the value of return for their investors.

ONE OF THE BIG IDEAS of business management which was utterly absent in state government is the holistic enterprise, where all players work together to increase value as a measure of success. As the chief of operations, Lientz believed the government was not constrained in its capability to be an effective enterprise.

"We determined that there is absolutely no reason that any government cannot and should not function with a high level of accountability and responsiveness to its citizens. There was no reason government decisions couldn't be facts-based; no reason government budgets should not follow policy and not vice versa; and no reason government should not treat citizens as customers, be willing to be accountable to them and to provide them with high levels of service delivery."

While Perdue does not see major differences in the challenges of managing a large public enterprise versus a large private enterprise, one distinction stands out. That is the dynamic of free enterprise, a system motivated, he suggests, by "the fear of failure and reward of success."

"That's what makes businesses hone their skills and management processes which deliver value to their customers, and therefore get more profit and return on investment to their shareholders. When you have been in that arena, it's real. You don't have the opportunity to be sloppy or make mistakes on an on-going basis. Capitalism holds us accountable for our actions and outcomes. That is the perspective I wanted within state government to give us the sense of accountability – not for the profit motive, but the value motive."

Bringing agency administrators – turf-masters of the bureaucracy – around to the enterprise view was a challenge, Perdue said. For one thing, it imposed a standard of accountability for proving value with empirical evidence, which made more work for managers. And it meant giving up some of the controls that protected the semi-autonomous "silo system."

THE "SILO SYSTEM" IS THE ANTITHESIS OF "THE ENTERPRISE." It is an anti-system. Government-wide systems like personnel administration, procurement and financial management were divvied in pieces and parts among agencies, resulting in overlapping ownership and inconsistent practices. "Back office" processes were being duplicated 80-something times by individual agencies, most of which were devising different ways of doing common functions. Fragmented, disaggregated data that is disembodied from shared systems defeats access and degrades accuracy. Consequently, the government loses the advantages of deploying resources where most needed, of leveraging economies of scale and of fostering collaboration among agencies with related issues. The state's operational culture increasingly gets in the way of success and works against managing to performance benchmarks.

Perdue found the silo mentality a major barrier to principles of good management and of delivering good government to citizens.

"It builds firewalls between agencies, which creates an unhealthy competition regarding appropriations and allocations. People are suspicious about sharing ideas, personnel and resources. Oftentimes there is a myopic view of roles, specifically as they relate to synergistic ways that could enhance effectiveness. The truth is, we are serving the same people... you look at the best overall for the whole, not the best for each individual agency."

CFO Tommy Hills described the fiscal situation he found as "dysfunctional."

The state had not produced a timely Consolidated Annual Financial Report in 15 years. His top concern was maintaining the state's prized AAA bond rating, a vote of confidence in the stability and soundness of fiscal management. Georgia was one of only seven states with straight A's from all rating agencies, but those scores are re-evaluated annually. How Georgia rebounded from recession and rebuilt its reserves would be a reckoning factor in the future.

Other enterprise-wide management areas – chief among them real estate matters – were bordering on chaotic. "It was clear that property was screwed up, because four different agencies were involved," Hills said. The Building Authority ran Capitol Hill, the State Properties Commission managed owned real estate, and the Department of Administrative Services handled leases. The Georgia State Financing and Investment Commission did the bidding for construction of new and renovated space.

"They didn't talk to each other," Hills said. "So if the Department of Corrections needed a parole office, they may go rent one, not knowing there was space available in a state building."

The Governor said he began to see clearly "where a critical mass of more centralized services could focus on specific processes, provide more consistent quality and outcomes, and relieve the agencies of administrative functions they didn't need to support."

FROM THE GOVERNOR'S NOTEPAD...
Visualize an enterprise model; identify areas for shared services.

WHY MANAGEMENT MATTERS

"Private business has the accountability of reporting on a 90-day cycle. There is no cycle in government, no interim accountability. The bureaucracy thinks it can muddle through, absent accountability and metrics. There was no thought process that there's a better way to do what we do."

JIM LIENTZ, CHIEF OPERATING OFFICER

Bureaucracy, in some respects, is an organization too big to fail. The consequences of state government collapsing are unimaginable and will not be allowed to happen, whatever it takes. Witness California and Illinois.

CHIEFS OF STATE

Chief Operating Officer Jim Lientz (*left*) and Chief Financial Officer Tommy Hills (*right*) brought top-level corporate leadership experience to the executive team. Governor Perdue's appointments of Georgia's first chiefs of operations and finance shifted the Administration's governing emphasis from political issues to performance-based management.

Keeping the massive operations of a mammoth bureaucracy in good working order is a painstaking job, but the neglecting of it brings a world of hurt. The state's functional infrastructure is like the undersides of bridges or buried water mains, out of sight and mind until something breaks or blows. Then everybody jumps on the costly consequences of deferred maintenance.

Like deferred maintenance, deferred management exacts a high price at the worst time, under the duress of declining revenues, trying to figure out after the fact how to do more with less. In 2008, that happened with shocking suddenness. Bureaucratic machinery isn't wired to downshift smoothly or swiftly.

That's what Governor Perdue means by "You can't immediately prepare for a crisis."

Many Governors see problems that need to be fixed. Perdue saw the invisible structure of a broken system, and he realized until it was redesigned and reconstructed, it would continue to be the source of costly inefficiencies. He also saw synergy in a hybrid system where bureaucracy embraced the innovations and incentives that spur results in private enterprise, albeit for the motive of value, not profit.

As America deals with the consequences of failure to manage well, states are paying greater attention to how they're minding the store. Management is moving from what John Watson called the "second tier" of governing to a more prominent priority.

The hard-learned takeaway from the recession of 2003, when Georgia was sliding into debt without a net, was that management could no longer be deferred as a priority of the Governor. Perdue immediately began the process of organizing the executive and administrative leadership to work as a team and think as an enterprise.

The next step would be to systematically re-engineer the bureaucratic machinery to run leaner operations, support value-based decisions about the use of resources and be prepared to respond expeditiously to changing conditions with the least negative impact on citizens.

It would require more than tweaking and tinkering with mechanics. It takes a transformation of the mindset of the leadership and the heart of the public service workforce – the culture of government.

BEGINNING WITH THE END IN MIND, Perdue found his goal: Georgia will be the Best-Managed State in America.

This mega-billion-dollar enterprise of the State of Georgia unquestionably held untold potential for cost savings and unrealized opportunities for improved service. The question was how to get at it. Real change rarely happens as an inside job. Breaking through administrative layers to core issues would take the right wedge, a driving force of fresh eyes and ideas focused on key functional areas from a corporate operations perspective.

"Business has benchmarks that they are valued on an ongoing basis in an economic way and a civic rent way, and that's Wall Street and the markets," Perdue explains. "Governments don't have that, so we need independent assessments to let us know how we're doing and to hold ourselves up in a transparent fashion that way."

Even with years of business experience, the Governor wasn't an expert on all the complex and technology-driven aspects of state operations. But he knew where to find the experts.

"We've got about 15 Fortune 500 businesses headquartered in our state," Perdue said. "We went to them because although you can't run government like a business, you can use principles at work in that marketplace and the best practices to give value. And as we give value in many different ways, our citizens are beneficiaries."

———

"How does value translate in a non-profit enterprise like the State of Georgia? Value is in areas like procurement and other areas where you reduce costs, leaving more money to invest in those things we know will bring dividends, like education. So it really was like an investment, we were harvesting the value from better efficiencies and better processes and investing the revenue back into things we knew would benefit all."

SONNY PERDUE, GOVERNOR OF GEORGIA

PRIVATE PARTNERS IN THE PUBLIC ENTERPRISE: A MODEL FOR SMART GOVERNMENT

The Commission for A New Georgia was chartered to engage the state's robust business sector in a public-private partnership to make Georgia the "best-managed state in America."

A non-profit corporation, privately funded and free of politics, the Commission amassed an amazing brain-trust from businesses, professions and academia. This was the New Georgia's idea factory, generating innovative thinking about how government can work better.

Nothing was random in the Commission's organization and operation. The design and development were deliberate in creating a business model for the organization, bringing the right people to the table and running a disciplined, sustainable project management system. Nearly 400 citizens from across the state invested time and expertise to improve their government. It worked productively for seven years, compiling an unprecedented record of results.

This is how it was done.

PART I: BLUEPRINT FOR A PUBLIC/PRIVATE BUSINESS MODEL

LEVERAGING VALUE: HOW TO BEST INVEST $950K

WE'RE NOT IN THE BLUE-RIBBON BUSINESS

PART II: THE ARCHITECTURE AND THE BUILDERS

A COMMISSION OF CORPORATE STATESMEN

THE COMMISSION CULTURE

FORCES EQUAL TO THE TASK

"I don't think the public understands the breadth, the wide scope and complexities of government. It's a complex system, and whoever is running it must have the skill set and a good grasp on what should take place – and then what elements are necessary to make those things really happen."

CARL SWEARINGEN, CHAIR OF PERDUE TRANSITION TEAM, 2003

Government is messy business. For the most part, Americans have preferred not to see what goes on inside the lawmaking sausage factory nor make a civic duty of probing the guts of government to examine its inner workings. A blogger's comment pegged the point: "I don't have the time or need to know how a TV or computer or government works. I just want it to work."

So bureaucratic machinery grinds on, operating in its own way in thousands of offices, behind counters and desks, in file drawers, on computer screens – in a world walled-off to the public and arcane to all but the innermost insiders. Even worker-bees are not always sure why they do what they do. Career employees watch the procession of governors passing through, and after each transitory term of change, homeostasis is restored, and business-as-usual is back on its feet.

Two potentially disruptive dynamics are recently afoot in that world: 21st Century technology and testy taxpayers.

Pick any key government function, and "There's an app for that." Tools of technology are ever-more capable of tapping data in agency silos and relaying it into enterprise-level, information-management systems. Special-purpose software components plug into systems to apply data to specific tasks. The systems generate dynamic views of costs, spending, results, trend-lines and a database of other facts essential to managing assets, finances and personnel.

No large enterprise operates without them – except most governments. When experts looked into Georgia's toolbox, it was, on average, 20 years behind the cutting edge in managing major operational cost centers.

Such technology enables the Transparency Factor which officials talk about, but few have the tools to apply. That level of technology doesn't show up unbidden. It is implemented by deliberate decision, often with a steep front-end investment. Georgia, in fact, has been honing a new tool for spend analytics, which sees every purchase made within the state and its university system – billions of dollars spent from the pockets of individual offices.

TECHNOLOGY HAS ALSO BEEN BUSY AT WORK OUTSIDE GOVERNMENT, delivering inside-government information to the public. Media outlets and public internet sites have made thousands of state and federal records an open book with a searchable index. Anyone can now read the label on legislative sausage or the ledgers of program expenditures and disseminate the information everywhere. Taxpayers, once blind, are getting an eyeful.

The calamities visited on Americans since 2008 have galvanized citizen interest in the way government runs its business and spends its public capital. The People are getting it: Management matters. And they are asking questions about who's minding the store.

But back in 2003, when Governor Sonny Perdue announced his goal to make Georgia the best-managed state in America, the silence was broken only by a gaping yawn across the citizenry, the media and the legislature.

PART I: BLUEPRINT FOR A PUBLIC/PRIVATE BUSINESS MODEL

LEVERAGING VALUE: HOW TO BEST INVEST $950K

"It's not the sexy, marquee political issues that affect everyday lives of citizens. Oftentimes, we in politics are seduced into aiming for big declarations, trying to leave a legacy. If I can leave a legacy of adding value to this state by good management and oversight of Georgia's public enterprise into the future, I will feel I have done what the people hired me to do."

GOVERNOR SONNY PERDUE

As a candidate in 2002, Sonny Perdue barely raised $3 million to unseat an incumbent governor of the majority party, who outspent Perdue almost 7-1. What a difference an election day makes.

In the aftermath of November 5, the Perdue team created the typical organization to "ensure the smooth and orderly transition from the former Governor's administration to the Governor-elect's administration." One of its duties was to mount a fundraising campaign to cover costs of the transition and inaugural activities with private money. Contributions and ticket sales poured in – $2.4 million in the two months up to inauguration day, January 13, 2003.

More than half of the funds picked up expenses for the transition team's preparations to make the new Administration ready for business on day one. Among their responsibilities were vetting qualified applicants for staff appointments, developing legislative, governmental and policy agendas, putting together the amended FY03 and FY04 budgets and setting up housekeeping in the Governor's Office.

When the transition's staffing and operating bills were paid at the end of January, 2003, the organization had almost $950,000 left in the bank.

"The Governor wanted to make sure those funds were used wisely in a way that would help the state grow and be beneficial to the citizens rather than building a war chest for the next campaign," said transition chairman Carl Swearingen. "There were a number of different possibilities discussed about having a commission or council or hiring consultants."

The decision would make a significant statement about the new Governor's principles and priorities. Putting the money where his message was, how could $950,000 be invested to get the most bang for the buck in a value proposition for Georgia?

The optimum use was suggested by the purpose that generated the contributions. Let's follow the money. On November 12, 2002, the Perdue Transition for A New Georgia had been incorporated by the Secretary of State as a non-profit civic organization "which is coordinating the transition of administrations from Roy Barnes to Sonny Perdue as Governor of Georgia." It was designated for federal tax-exempt status under the 501(c) (4) definition of "social welfare organizations." Its qualification was affirmed by the IRS, based on the precedent of rulings which allowed the same exemption for the U.S. Presidential transitions of Clinton-Gore and Bush-Cheney.

Corporate status allowed the Perdue Transition to "acquire, establish, retain and maintain funds to be held, invested and used exclusively for the purposes of organizing and carrying on the various activities and events associated with the transition of administrations." The officers of the corporation were transition chair Swearingen, vice chair John Watson and secretary Glenda Garris. On November 15, the name was officially re-registered as the Transition for A New Georgia, with the same officers. "New Georgia" had been the Perdue campaign theme, the promise of a new approach to the business of government – principle-centered, customer-focused, facts-based and results-driven.

During the two-month fund appeal, the business community responded to the call for building a climate of support and a strong start for the new Governor. In the campaign, a majority of major-league corporate donors had put their money on the other guy. Now Sonny Perdue was the leader who would drive the state's progress for the next four years. Georgia-based companies were big stakeholders in that enterprise.

"Georgia's business community has always been committed to the continued economic vitality of our state. Promoting a positive economic climate, enhancing the quality of life and improving our state's educational system have always been priorities," said Chief of Staff Eric Tanenblatt. "While many in the business community supported the Governor's opponent in the election, they rallied around the new governor and offered their assistance."

Any funds remaining after the transition could be distributed to other qualifying organizations by decision of the officers if the original entity were dissolved. Or the funds could be rolled over to a related corporate purpose by amending the articles.

THE MONTHS BETWEEN ELECTION AND INAUGURATION WERE CRAZY-BUSY. New staff members were coming aboard, bringing their ideas to gel the concept of a "New Georgia." The business-like mindset was a definite paradigm of the thinking. Chief among the thought leaders was transition chair Swearingen, who had recently retired as senior vice president and corporate secretary of the BellSouth Corporation. He was no novice in the leadership circles of government. He had been tapped before by governors to serve on statewide commissions, and he was Perdue's first choice to spearhead the transition. Swearingen organized the strategic areas for policy and progress into five categories: health, education, economic growth, safety and redefining government. These were adopted as the broad organizing themes for administration initiatives and objectives.

Tanenblatt believed that the Governor's focus on the role of CEO – talking a language business people understand – would resonate with the state's corporate constituency.

The appointment of Jim Lientz as chief of state operations scored early points for credibility. Swearingen said Lientz's involvement signaled externally "that we were trying to insure we have the best people available running this multi-billion dollar operation."

While the idea of Georgia becoming America's "best-managed state" may have been a snoozer to most citizens, the business sector would "get it" as a visionary goal.

"Coming from the private sector, the Governor recognized that there were business practices that could easily be applied to the public sector to make government more efficient," Tanenblatt said. "Governor Perdue wanted to engage the talent of the private sector to assist in identifying and applying business principles to specific areas in state government."

The elements of a commission were fitting hand in glove:

- There was an existing incorporated organization with a substantial account of operating funds.

- The Governor's mission to create a best-managed state was congruent with the Section 501 "social welfare" objectives of better government.

- The rallying of business support created a receptive constituency for a private-sector, non-political advisory body to focus on applying smart management strategies, current technologies, best practices and industry standards to state operations – the necessities of a best-managed state.

What was not to like? On January 31, 2003, Swearingen and Garris passed the baton of their offices in the Transition for A New Georgia, Inc. to John Watson as president and Fred Cooper, head of a private investment firm, as secretary-treasurer. These officers would organize the changeover to the Commission for A New Georgia. Watson said the way the Commission was established carried out a deliberate design for its effectiveness.

> "The excess revenue from the transition could have been spent on lots of different political things. We had saved resources by running the business of the transition efficiently, and we made a commitment to put them into a project which would accomplish that for government.

> "We did not want the Commission to be a flash in the pan. The whole purpose of the appropriation was meant to give it sustainability and longevity, since historically those types of 'blue-ribbon, good-government' commissions are episodic. I think when the business community understood there was a long-term commitment to asking the right questions, that was stage one.

> "The next stage is the commitment to execution. My belief is that when people see the accumulation of a process and not just shelving the process after brainstorming, then people feel the reward that their time is valuable. Especially if you are a volunteer, you want to feel your time is valued. The only way to show that is in execution."

Between January and June 2003, the corporation began to define and acquire the structure and leadership of a Commission built to last through the foreseeable future of a four-year term.

WE'RE NOT IN THE BLUE-RIBBON BUSINESS

"The thought was always for an action commission, not a research project. The job was not to diagnose problems and leave the prescription to someone else. This was a triage… a SWAT team… a therapy approach to the most visible problems we needed to deal with to reach our vision."

GOVERNOR SONNY PERDUE

The Governor's message to Commission organizers was writ large: This would NOT be one more in a series of "blue-ribbon, all-analysis-no-action" ventures.

"The Governor was clear from the outset that he did not want to form a committee that would spend a year coming up with notebooks and reams of paper that would collect dust on a shelf," Tanenblatt said.

The Governor's instructions, he recalled, were to think of task forces "like SWAT teams" which would target problem areas, get a scope on practical solutions for improvement and pull the trigger on recommendations for action.

"We wanted to go after specific problems and specific solutions that could be implemented in real time," Tanenblatt said. "To keep things fresh and constantly look for ways to be more effective and efficient, it would warrant an ongoing initiative."

Running the Commission like a business was a given. The corporation structure would emulate the way executives work in their own companies. The business model was designed for effective use of the leaders' valuable time, efficient project management to expedite decision-making and accountability reports on results. The CEO – the Governor – would attend all board meetings.

The corporate articles were in place for fiduciary accountability, transactions and expenditures, monthly accounting reports, annual audits, bylaws and indemnity. No board directors or members would be compensated. Funds were designated for limited staff, office and communications equipment (computers, Blackberries, phones), supplies, leased space in a government building, a public website, corporate insurance, and accounting and auditing services. In the initial months, funds also paid for consulting assistance to set up the project management system and get multiple task forces up and running on a clockwork timeline.

The legal work to establish the corporation was handled pro bono by the firm of King and Spalding. Every detail was nailed down. This was no loosey-goosey operation that could expose the Commission members or Governor to risk.

THE LEADERSHIP OF THE COMMISSION was carefully considered. The Governor knew he wanted "a Commission of statesmen and leaders of action."

"I was focused on getting chairmen who did not have a specific political agenda, who had high expectations, and who were people of action," said Perdue. "I didn't want people who would talk solutions to death."

The chosen co-chairs were impressively connected, highly respected leaders from different sectors of the business community. Joe Rogers, President and CEO of Waffle House, stood tall in the circle of CEOs who occupy the headquarters of international corporations based in Atlanta. Rogers earned degrees from Georgia Tech and Harvard and served on high-profile foundations. Bob Hatcher, CEO of MidCountry Financial and Georgia Chairman of BB&T, was a University of Georgia graduate and a pillar of Macon's leadership establishment, with a distinguished record of appointments and affiliations. He was serving as chairman of the Georgia Chamber of Commerce, which kept him in touch with a statewide network of diverse businesses.

"Both brought unique strengths to the table," Swearingen said. "We had two leaders with a passion for continuous improvement and with a demonstration of this effort in their careers."

Hatcher said the co-chairs' brainstorming sessions on prospective Commission members produced a "beautiful blend of small and large businesses from Atlanta and other communities. We were deliberately trying to put business diversity, as well as ethnicity and gender representation, on the Commission."

Rogers and Hatcher had been approached separately by the Governor about leading the Commission. They later discovered that each had asked the same question of Perdue before agreeing to co-chair. Hatcher recalls his own words as, "Are you really going to do anything with all this work?"

"I told the Governor it was going to take a lot of time, but it wouldn't be a waste of time if he intended to implement recommendations. His answer was, 'Yes.'"

Hatcher and Rogers themselves had to answer that question time and again as they invited busy executives to serve on the Commission. "They did want to help. They did not want to waste their time," Hatcher said.

EXACTLY WHAT THE COMMISSION WAS GOING TO BE DOING was a bit open-ended beyond the idea that task forces would be formed to examine business operations and recommend best practices to improve performance.

Focusing on the "doing" was Annie Hunt Burris, deputy chief of staff, who had served on Governor Zell Miller's 1991 Commission for Efficiency and Effectiveness in Government. She came to the Perdue Administration from the University System of Georgia where she was associate vice chancellor of economic development programs. She had also worked in

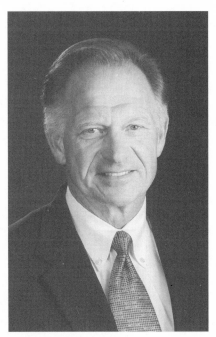

"TWO LEADERS WITH A PASSION FOR CONTINUOUS IMPROVEMENT"

Bob Hatcher (*left*) and Joe Rogers (*right*) brought distinctive strengths to their roles as CNG co-chairs. Their selection represented the spectrum of Georgia's business-sector leadership and personified Governor Perdue's idea of "a Commission of statesmen who have high expectations and are people of action."

economic planning for private and public organizations. Her conversations with the Governor about identifying a Perdue legacy always turned to the same vision.

"What the Governor wanted to accomplish in his term was to change the culture of government," Burriss said. "That was the challenge he threw to us in the policy area. And I'm thinking, 'How do we do that in tangible way?'"

"From an operational standpoint," she said, "we were trying to figure out how to cut budgets. It was obvious to me that the state of Georgia had no idea about its assets, how many vehicles it owned or its real estate. I knew that from my economic development days.

"I had served on Governor Miller's Williams Commission, which had looked at many of the same issues we were dealing with a decade later. I knew how that commission had worked, and what was and was not effective.

"The main thing that was effective was connecting people with good ideas who could make things happen."

Burriss believed the tangibles would come from a hands-on plan "to re-engineer the government structure with private-sector practices that are better geared to leverage funds for effective outcomes." She added to that the catalyst of "cutting-edge thinking to examine issues with fresh perspective." She was a big believer that dollars saved through better management were like "found" money. "That's the best kind, because it doesn't come from raising taxes."

THE WORKHORSES OF THE COMMISSION would be the short-term, rotating task forces, and that would require securing a commitment of personnel from key companies. Burriss knew where the major players would be found.

> "I started thinking of great firms who had people they wouldn't dare let go on loan, but might let them participate if we asked for their help with some of our issues. I just started going around to executives who had a lot of expertise in different areas and getting ideas of topical issues we could tackle. From there, I drew out a timeline to show how we could do this in tiers. We could do task forces in quarters, three at a time, and overlap them. Most executives will do things if you set a time limit. We said, 'Ninety days and you're done.'
>
> "In order to get to 90 days, you only had to attend three meetings. If you wanted a real high-level individual, that was the only way. So it was three meetings, three months. In 90 days you submit a report. Every quarter the Commission kicks off new groups."

On task forces, size matters, Burriss said. "UPS had done studies about organizational development and learned the most effective committees were no bigger than eight. It's like a successful dinner party. Beyond that number, human dynamics change, since some members won't speak up if you have more than that in the room."

The Governor actually had a task force underway in a separate arena, and he was eyeing it as a prototype for the Commission. In January 2003, Perdue had appointed a 14-member public/private task force, chaired by Georgia Tech President Wayne Clough. Their task was to make recommendations for a cost-effective proposal to manage telecommunications and computing services for the state. The plan would impact enterprise-wide, mission-critical capabilities tied to rapidly advancing technologies. The issue was a holdover from a Barnes initiative, still on the table when Perdue took office. The state's largest-ever outsourcing contract – $1.8 billion over 10 years – had come down to one bidder left standing. At stake were the takeover of Georgia's IT operations and the development of a new communications network for government offices and school systems. Perdue wanted the contract and bidding situation reviewed by a panel of experts before a decision was made. (At the end, the task force voted thumbs down.)

Perdue was impressed by the task force's knowledge base, methodology and thoroughness. Members brought a breadth of expertise from academia, industry and government. The impeccable credibility of its chairman was critical to the outcome. The task force committees met with scores of agency representatives, industry providers and IT managers to probe a full spectrum of perspectives. They analyzed costs, benefits and risks. And they delivered straightforward recommendations on a short timeline.

Clough praised Perdue for his "bold approach" in enlisting outside experts to help solve a complex problem for the state. Clough said the task force's flexible and strategic approach would result in "significant savings to the state as well as offer an opportunity for considerably enhanced efficiencies in state services."

These were the words the Governor wanted to hear. He saw in action the model and outcomes he envisioned for Commission for A New Georgia task forces: short-term, impactful, expert-driven work groups which deliver specific, actionable recommendations.

IN THE CHANGEOVER of the corporation to the Commission for A New Georgia, King & Spalding's counsel sought IRS approval of the broadened mission:

> The organization… has shifted its focus toward making Georgia one of the best-managed states in the nation. To bring creativity and innovation from the private sector into the effort to improve Georgia state government, the organization will create a number of small working groups or task forces to cover a variety of major study areas. Each task force will focus in depth on one of the study areas identified by the organization. Prominent Georgia business leaders recruited by the organization will lead

and serve on the working groups. Each task force will work diligently and for a relatively short period of time to delve into an issue and to generate ideas for adapting best practices from the private sector into the area of study. The creative ideas generated by each task force will be forwarded as recommendations to the Governor and members of his leadership team.

The IRS approved, and the Commission for A New Georgia was in business.

PART II: THE ARCHITECTURE AND THE BUILDERS

A COMMISSION OF CORPORATE STATESMEN

"Let me be clear. We're not looking for ideas about how to maintain an average level of performance. We're looking for Commission members to suggest ideas for attaining the same high performance corporations aspire to. We're aiming for Georgia to be recognized as one of the nation's best-managed states by 2007."

GOVERNOR SONNY PERDUE, ANNOUNCING THE COMMISSION FOR A NEW GEORGIA

The Governor chose a ready-made audience for staging the announcement of a business-led commission to improve government. It was the 2003 Spring Retreat of the Georgia State Chamber of Commerce in May, and the new Governor was the keynoter. Many of the people in the audience would later become part of the Commission's working relationship with the state's business community.

The Governor's Office press release, datelined Atlanta, May 23, 2003, gave the short take in the subhead: "Innovative Task Forces Will Bring Private-Sector Expertise and Approach to Government Issues."

Perdue's quote touched all the key words: "The Commission provides an ideal opportunity for committed Georgians from the private sector to lend their expertise in areas of policy development and governmental operations. I fully expect that the Commission model for continuous improvement will become an integrated part of the culture of governing and providing services for the people of Georgia."

Perdue also said strong private-sector leadership would be essential in re-forming state government "by challenging the old ways of doing business and

CHARTER MEMBERS OF THE COMMISSION FOR A NEW GEORGIA

Dan Amos, President and CEO of Aflac, Inc.

Arthur Blank, Home Depot founder, Falcons owner and Chairman of The Arthur M. Blank Family Foundation

Robert Brown, President and CEO of R. L. Brown & Associates, Inc.

Anna Cablik, President of Anatek, Inc. and Anasteel Supply

John Cay, Chairman and CEO, Palmer and Cay insurance

Steve Heyer, President and COO of The Coca-Cola Company

Bill Jones III, Chairman and CEO of The Sea Island Company

Frank Jones, Retired Partner, King & Spalding

Wyck Knox, Partner in Kilpatrick Stockton

Dink NeSmith, President of Community Newspapers, Inc.

Neal Purcell, Retired Managing Partner of KPMG

David Ratcliffe, President and CEO, The Georgia Power Company

Robert Ratliff, Founder and CEO of AGCO

John Rice, President and CEO of GE Power Systems

Ray Robinson, Former AT&T President of the Southern Region

Paula Rosput, Chairman, President and CEO of AGL Resources, Inc.

Roy Rowland, M.D., retired Congressman

Carl Swearingen, Chair of the Perdue Transition Team, retired Senior Vice Chairman and Corporate Secretary of BellSouth

Rick Ussery, Chairman and CEO of TSYS

Phillip Wilheit, President of Wilheit Packaging

encouraging new ideas and strategies for governing our state."

He announced Hatcher and Rogers as CNG co-chairs. Bill Todd, past president of the Georgia Research Alliance, then on loan to Perdue's staff, was appointed executive director.

The press release outlined the plan to recruit "prominent Georgia business leaders" to chair task forces of small, highly focused working groups created around 12 to 15 major themes. A Commission member would shadow each task force. Their task was to analyze an operational area of government, learn everything possible about the issues, assess findings and recommend actions for improvement. Their report would be presented by the task force chair at a quarterly Commission meeting, heard firsthand by the CNG board, the Governor and his chiefs of operating and finance. The recommendations would be reviewed and assigned to the "owner" agency for implementation with accountability.

The story concluded with a promise by the Governor to bring a "new twist" to government:

> "Although there is no difference in the amount of dedication to excellence between the private and public sectors, government operations often have been plagued by large, long-standing bureaucracies that didn't facilitate the creation or implementation of new or better approaches to problems. The nimble, strategic make-up of the Commission will address these historic barriers and bring a new 'twist' to how Georgia operates."

A month later, on June 26, 2003, a follow-up release from the Governor's Office heralded the newly appointed Commission board. It was an A-list of 20 high-profile executives representing a mix of international blue-chip corporations and highly successful Georgia-founded companies. The members fit the Governor's measure for a "Commission of statesmen" who would bring the perspective of their distinguished careers to the challenges of the state enterprise.

Among the Commission's charter class, John Rice of GE said that while the mechanics of government were not an area of his expertise, he was "intrigued with the idea" of the private-sector collaboration with government in creating a best-managed state. He readily saw not only the advantage of a business approach to government operations, but also the credibility that a business-led commission would leverage in change-making decisions.

> "I felt we would be able to bring in successful ideas from the private sector. I also thought we would be helpful in reinforcing the need to make the difficult calls and be an independent sounding board in the vetting process. Situations like department reorganization are tough no matter what sector you're in. We would provide independent confirmation of what the Governor knew they needed to do."

Over the years, a handful of members would bow off the board and new appointments take their seats. When the Commission closed its books in 2010, 16 of the original members had stayed the course to the last meeting.

THE COMMISSION CULTURE

"This is not the old Georgia; it's not the Georgia that many of us grew up in and worked in for many years. It requires a new focus in how we look at things and how we do things. This is exactly where the business focus and the business expertise of the Commission for A New Georgia have come together."
JIM LIENTZ, CHIEF OPERATING OFFICER, STATE OF GEORGIA

The Commission for A New Georgia – the state's first commission of the 21st Century – had some old business to take care of, as well as an agenda of new business. This wasn't the first commission to engage private-sector partners in a mission of government reform, but it intended to be the altogether new and improved model for doing that business.

The last reform event was Governor Zell Miller's 1991 Commission on Effectiveness and Economy and Government. It was dubbed the "Williams Commission" for its chairman Virgil Williams, a land developer who was Miller's campaign manager and later his chief of staff. Like CNG, the Williams Commission was launched in a recession, with a priority on reducing the cost of government. Miller said the commission's charge went beyond "eliminating waste." Its purpose, he said, was "streamlining and restructuring administrative overhead to shift our focus to service delivery." The result, according to Miller, was to be not just a "slimmed-down bureaucracy," but a government more effective in providing high-quality services to the people of Georgia."

Nearly 60 Georgians in business and government collaborated on 13 task forces and delivered an 800-page report to Miller a year later. More than a decade after the Williams report laid out a detailed plan of bureaucratic reform, many of the same issues were back on CNG's table, unchanged.

This was the fate of generations of similar attempts to re-engineer government operations, going back to Governor Richard B. Russell in 1931. Governor Jimmy Carter's 1971 Reorganization and Management Improvement Study produced a 2,500-page volume of recommendations. Carter called their proposals "the best...we could put together to make state government more responsive to Georgia citizens and to produce maximum economy and efficiency in government." Many of those recommendations were passed along as unfinished business to the Williams Commission 20 years later.

Before Carter, Governor Carl Sanders had tried his hand with the Commission for Efficiency and Improvement in Government, chaired by William Bowdoin. Again, the brainpower of Georgia's brightest and best public and private servants was trained on obvious problems – in Bowdoin's words, "money being spent uselessly because of lack of centralized planning and frequent duplication of administrative machinery."

IN THE HISTORICAL SHADOW OF ITS PREDECESSORS, the Commission for A New Georgia faced similar challenges as its organizational meeting was convened June 27, 2003.

Georgia Tech President Wayne Clough was called in to talk about how a successful task force operates. His leadership of the Governor's technology committee had established the prototype for the Commission. Clough went through 16 points, which Co-chair Joe Rogers wrote down and kept as his "rules of the road." (As a footnote, Clough left a celebrated presidency at Tech to become the Secretary of the Smithsonian Institution in 2008.)

Clough's basics were commonsensical, but essential: strong emphasis on clear, well-defined tasks and expectations for outcomes; prescribed communications procedures; pre-briefings of everyone invited to meetings; and specified deadlines for deliverables to assure participants of an end-point. Clough also addressed open records, encouraging publication of minutes, openness to interviews with media and a development of a public website for reports. He advised the Commission to "avoid negative messages" about past practices – to keep a positive focus on the future.

At the meeting, Co-chair Joe Rogers described (and underestimated) CNG's horizon as a two-year process, organized around quarterly meetings of the whole with several task forces at work during each quarter. The Commission members were asked to sign up for one of the five "councils" which would become the guiding groups for the Governor's themes for making Georgia healthier, more educated, safer, growing and a best-managed state. Co-chair Bob Hatcher passed out a list of 18 potential task force topics and asked members to vote for their top five picks to help prioritize the list.

The Governor stepped up to formally charge the Commission, reiterating that their venture was indeed a serious undertaking, backed by his personal pledge to "not waste your time." He asked the members to see his vision of a transformed culture for Georgia government – better-managed, customer-focused and strategically working to expand opportunities for the state. Meeting minutes summarized Perdue's talking points:

- The Commission's view is from the 100,000-foot level, taking in the big picture of where the state needs to be moving. Flushing out issues and solutions would take place in the smaller task forces.

- Outside stimulus is needed to generate new ideas and initiate management change. "This is not a blue-ribbon panel," Perdue is quoted. "We expect action, deliverables, and the Governor to be held accountable for results."

- Commitment and perseverance are essential to culture reform. "State government is embedded in a bureaucracy that resists change. Innovation needs to be infused throughout government." Focus on strategy and action: "Think of state government as a delivery model for services."

- State employees need identification of goals that stretch their motivation. "We need to inspire people to do the work of improvement."

- Leadership development is key, because organizations are built on people. "State government is not good at providing career paths for people who want to make a difference. We can learn from Fortune 500 companies which do it best."

Perdue also re-affirmed his pledge to "not do a thick book that would become a doorstop. I've bought into the things that we could do better, and we are committed to do that."

CNG Executive Director Bill Todd pointed out that becoming a "Best-Managed State" was not a mythical goal. Since 1999, the Pew Center for the States had been conducting management evaluations for their triennial Government Performance report card. State governments were graded in four areas of performance: Money, People, Infrastructure and Information. In the 2001 ratings, Georgia had rated a B-minus – the average score. The 2004 study, then underway, would barely reflect a year's work in the Perdue Administration. The next round after that in 2007 would coincide with the end of the Governor's first term. The Commission's goal was to upgrade Georgia's rating to an "A" by then. Typically only two to four of the 50 states make the A list at all.

COMMISSION MEMBERS LEFT THE MEETING with several themes in mind and a handful of seeds for future task forces. Rogers said culture change stood out. "It wasn't just about changing business processes. It was, 'Can we change the culture; can we deal with the embedded bureaucracy; can the state be held accountable?' The Governor talked about state employees' attitude and role. That's where the initiatives for customer service and leadership task forces ultimately came up."

Rogers said that the logistics of holding the quarterly meetings at the Governor's Mansion with the Governor always in attendance was an incentive for members to show up, acknowledging, "We couldn't keep it going without that." The group had also agreed to a sequential process for the work. "Don't tee off all the ideas at once – do a few, finish those, do a few more, finish, and so on." It was a dynamically different approach from previous commissions which worked for a year or more and delivered a forklift of recommendations all at once.

Hatcher detected no inclination for grandstanding by the Commission members or the Governor. The motto, he said, was to "under-promise and over-deliver. Don't talk about what you're going to do. Talk about what you've done."

"The visibility of the Commission in the public eye wasn't a priority, and we didn't try to go there," Hatcher insisted. "All visibility does is give people something to shoot at. The visibility within state government that we were effecting change was there, so we didn't need to be outside."

Basically, Hatcher said, the Governor was asking experienced executives to analyze the operations of government as if it were their own business and recommend what they would do to improve performance.

"What did we know about the management situation of the state government? We didn't know enough to be scared," Rogers admitted. "We weren't worrying about embedded bureaucracy because we hadn't dealt with it. You could laugh at jokes about 'government work,' but you realized, for the most part, state employees are well-intentioned people. There's a 9-to-5 mentality in a lot of people, and not just in government.

"Culture and process are two different things. Changing the process helps people look at how to do their jobs in a new way. But through customer service and leadership development, employees saw we weren't just focusing on process. There was attention to the people doing the work."

Hatcher also made the distinction between management and leadership and the need for both to work together.

"You manage things, and you lead people," Hatcher said. "In any organization both are vital. Management is stacking up things and getting them into systems and in some order. It's the leadership of people that changes culture. Leadership development is something larger businesses work on for years. It's really the future of your business to grow people and make them better capable of making their own decisions and leading others. That didn't exist in government."

ROGERS VOICED THE GENERAL VIEW of the Commission members that "with the right mindset of the leadership," state government could be run like a business on budget and delivery issues.

"You've got revenue, you've got costs, you've got customers," Rogers said. "Think about value creation for your customers – like saving time on getting a driver's license. You can go though every department and ask employees, 'Are we creating good customer value here, or are we just getting paid to annoy customers who have to put up with it because we have no competition?' You can't go to Walgreen's to get a driver's license. Sonny likes value for customers… it's tangible."

What does the business sector bring to the table for government? Said Rogers:

"All we bring is experience born of competition. Those of us in the private sector are no different than those in the public sector except for the environment we deal in. Competition forces us. Financial constraints force us. Our balance sheet and auditors require we know where all of our assets are. We couldn't get a clean audit if we didn't know where all of our real estate is. The state doesn't have to get a clean audit, and that's the risk. The State of Georgia is not going to have any in-state competition to force accountability. It comes from applying outside pressure and leadership from this Governor and the next and the next, with forward-looking processes, whether it's on things or people, and a constant interaction with the private sector to say, 'Are we doing as well as we could be doing?'"

The success of the Commission, Rogers felt, would be underwritten by the Executive Branch's commitment to a true public/private partnership.

"We had all the right people at the table. We weren't trying to go around the senior leadership," Rogers said. "The good news was that the Governor had great senior leadership. Jim Lientz and Tommy Hills were not wed to anything government-wise. The last thing they were was territorial. They were exploring the territory themselves. And they were glad to have the Commission throw a couple of the first punches."

FORCES EQUAL TO THE TASK

"The Commission never got over the line into policy where there would be a huge debate that focused on private-sector issues. You couldn't invite the hospital system in to fix health care. But it's okay for the bank guy to come in and focus on bond ratings."

JOE ROGERS, CO-CHAIR, COMMISSION FOR A NEW GEORGIA

The importance of the first wave of task forces went beyond the issues tackled and recommendations coming forth. Their groundwork established the organizational stature and qualitative standards that would secure credibility and continuity of CNG initiatives going forward.

Every element was crucial in the end-to-end process: topic selection, the right chair, composition of the task force, methodology of the work plan, quality of research and information, the dynamics of discussion, data-driven decision making, consensus for recommendations and format of the final presentation.

Topics. Although Commission members were being consulted on topics, it was understood that the initial list would come from the Governor's Office, based on the triage of operational issues that compromised sound management.

"Most of the ideas that came back to us from polls of the Commission members were more policy suggestions like education and healthcare," Hatcher recalled. "The Governor's staff said, 'These are fine, but we really need you to look at real estate or cars.' So we stopped polling people and got down to work."

Deputy Chief Burriss explained the hierarchy of issues that was emerging in the context of the times: "What can we do to resolve our financial situation? How do we manage our assets with good stewardship? How is state government organized to create good results? And how do we generate more revenue?"

The first task forces, she said, were about "tangible things" and ownership issues tied to them – space management, capital construction, fleet management and procurement. The state needed a handle on what it owned, the cost of ownership and who was minding the business. At the top of the list was Administrative Services, the big umbrella over the moving parts.

"Profitable companies have to keep their overhead down, and therefore develop good cost-management skills," Burriss said. "Cutting costs was also a high priority for the Governor. We had a good Venn diagram, where government and the private sector overlap."

The circumstances of recession also argued for exploration of ways to leverage public/private economic assets, such as tourism, more strategically.

As a Commission member, Swearingen was interested in getting started on the longer-term issue of leadership succession.

"Coming from the transition team, my first thought was leadership. If we're going to develop a New Georgia, we had to instill a sense of value and stewardship, then make sure there was some formal program underway, not only to develop leaders, but to identify those with potential." Leadership Development made the cut.

Task force chairs and members. Matching task force topics with the right chairperson would be a key determinant for an effective outcome. One of the most important tasks of the Commission members was to recruit team leadership.

"Recruiting focused on people who were highly capable," said Rogers. "It wasn't necessary to have a marquee name chairing the most visible task force. You looked for talent. Phil Humann was CEO and Chairman of SunTrust, and he chaired a task force in a relatively narrow area, seeking new options for financing capital projects. Donna Hyland chaired receivables. She was the COO of Children's Hospital, but she understood the process. Jim Balloun was CEO of Acuity Brands, which had just transformed their procurement process. Jim Carson had been CFO, COO and CEO of Carter Associates, a major commercial real estate firm. He knew capital projects."

The chairs of task forces were also selected for their clout – being the right person to ask the right person to be a member or a consultant. They were typically selected without clearance from the Governor. The choices never backfired.

As task force chairs were being enlisted, the search was also on for members to serve on each of the initial work groups. In summer 2003, Kris Nordholz, a young staffer from the Governor's office, was transferred to the Commission as deputy director to Bill Todd. His immediate job was identifying private-sector prospects for the task forces. Nordholz focused on expertise, diversity and citizenry.

"The process of recruiting was about involving all kinds of people," Nordholz said. His previous assignment in external affairs put him in touch with local Chambers of Commerce, faith-based groups, constituents who participated in Governor's events and the Perdue campaign network. The list was broad, but the qualifiers were specific.

"We built the task forces around the chair people, with seven to 10 or 11 members," Nordholz said. "I created a matrix of the task force make-up. We'd go for a number from different geographic regions, for women, for minorities, all with expertise."

Nordholz said local chambers were solid sources of referrals to particular types of business people. That often meant he was making cold calls to prospects he didn't know personally.

"A big challenge in recruiting was explaining what we were trying to do, since there were not a lot of specifics about how the first task forces would work," said Nordholz. "But it was actually relatively easy to get somebody on the phone and get a yes. When you call from the Governor's Office, they don't hang up on you."

From experience, COO Lientz said the defined, 90-day commitment helped prospects say yes. "The short duration implied decision-making to business folks. No one wanted to be part of a perpetual committee."

CONSULTANTS. Realistically, even the most experienced, expert task forces with the best leadership were limited in their time and tools to pull off a thorough analysis of complex bureaucratic operations. They all had high-pressure day jobs in different parts of the state. The quality of information gathered depended on focused fact-finding inside government, a broad knowledge of national trends in the field and tools for analyzing findings. That had to come from a separate team with special resources.

The Commission's biggest coup was in persuading the top consulting groups on the globe to commit their people as partners to the task forces. For free. They amassed a stunning private-sector portfolio: McKinsey, Deloitte, Accenture, Goldman-Sachs, Hewitt, North Highland, IBM, KPMG, Booz-Allen Hamilton, Ernst and Young, Bearing Point, Price-Waterhouse and the Kauffman Foundation.

State CFO Tommy Hills said the consultants put the stamp of "absolute excellence" on the task force product. This was a critical point in translating Commission recommendations to decision-making in the Governor's Office.

"There was no way we could have agreed on recommendations without the data and analysis they provided," said Hills. "They did millions of dollars worth of first-class work for free. They were incredibly valuable, great citizens of Georgia."

Burriss echoed the kudos, calling consultants "the unsung heroes for a lot of extraordinary work getting done." She cited the example of the Space Management Task Force, where Ann Cramer, director of IBM Corporate Citizenship and Corporate Affairs, stepped up. "You could call Ann and say, "I need this kind of help but we can't pay you," and she would agree. She is a great corporate citizen." IBM ultimately was consulting partner on two massive task force efforts: Space Management and Workforce Development.

Why would world-class consulting firms, which bill clients millions of dollars for such services, give it away to government?

Nordholz responds that for the first five-to-seven task forces, "Actually, it was not a hard sell. Calling from the Governor's Office got them interested. There was a new wave of energy around Governor Perdue, and when you're in the business of those firms, working with government has benefits. Well, I hope there was a business benefit at some point – but they all just wanted to help."

In addition to paying their civic rent in the spirit of public service, consulting firms can make profitable use of exemplar projects to market their expertise to future clients. Some projects lead to contract work to implement recommendations, and the consultants may hope for an inside track based on knowledge of the situation. Every consulting firm understood up front that there were no strings on CNG projects. The state contracting process is one of the most severely scrutinized transactions in government. Still, working at the highest level of government in one state can be a valuable reference for being hired to replicate the success in another public organization. And every learning experience builds on the consulting group's knowledge base. The trade-offs made business sense.

Joe Rogers explained that early successes in involving consulting firms begat a "process that fed on itself. You could leverage the fact that North Highland, Deloitte or KPMG gave us some pro bono time, and then others didn't want to be the one that said no. Also, they realized they had a fixed, focused commitment. They weren't being asked to deliver free goods on an open-ended basis."

PROCESS. At the same time Nordholz was seeking qualified task force members, the wheels were turning on how to set up a process that would work productively – even perfectly – in coordinating the players and phases of multiple task forces with overlapping timelines. The logistics were daunting, and the devil was in the details. Nordholz was sweating those details when an answer jumped out of his TV set into his lap.

> "I was sitting around one night, flipping channels and came across, on C-SPAN or public television, a panel talking about efficiency in government. I thought, 'God had a plan for the Commission!' I started watching and at one point, a guy from Deloitte spoke about organization, and I wrote down his name. I went to their website, found his bio and phone number and called him. He called back. I told him what we were doing, and he put us in touch with Deloitte in Atlanta. We paid them a small engagement fee to oversee the organization of the Commission and task forces. That's one of the biggest things we could leave behind."

Deloitte's public-sector practice is a star in both government reform and organizational innovation, the perfect fit for the CNG mission. In Fall 2003, as the first battery of task forces were beginning to form, Deloitte-Atlanta sent in Keith Waldrop to map out a process that shows "what the path to success looks like."

"The project was described to me as the need to streamline the process for kicking off the task forces, so when they were named and the start date hit, they would spend as little time as possible on administrative tasks to ramp up," Waldrop said. "I was told that we needed to 'turn this thing into a widget factory.'"

In other words, no piece of the process was left to guesswork or chance. Clarity, rigor and purpose were built into the overarching scheme.

The manual would cover every step in templates and tools: on-boarding new members; defining leadership and staff roles; deciding the scope of topic; planning each meeting agenda and activities; and guiding development of deliverables. Waldrop spent the first weeks studying the Deloitte methodologies for effective organization and processes to glean the pieces that fit the Commission. Phasing the work was a critical component of staying on the 90-day track with several task forces online at once.

The CNG planning guide grew to a notebook of nearly 200 pages outlining the methodology each task force would use to initiate, develop and finalize the project. A timeline laid out the major meetings and activities in a typical lifecycle. The activities were accelerated by a set of pre-designed tools in the notebook.

Meanwhile, in the background, Deloitte staff member Garry Fielding was piecing together hundreds of entries in a mural-sized mosaic of the state's current business model. Called "The Georgia Roadmap," nothing like it had ever been developed in state government. The matrix laid out the state's organizational structure by agency and budget, cross-matched with 57 of the state's major business processes. The color-coded spreadsheet clearly marked where different agencies overlapped in authority and duplications of functions and operations. Unfurled and mounted on the wall, it spanned more than six feet.

"The map was a visual tool to facilitate an understanding of the structure of state government at the enterprise level," Waldrop said. "It helped the Commission and task forces identify opportunities and suggest recommendations to improve the way the state conducts business." The map was rolled out for the kickoff of task force meetings to help newbies get their bearings in the labyrinth of bureaucracy.

Improvement opportunities would include cost savings, efficiencies, shared services, world-class customer service and better opportunities for the state's employees.

A website was developed to give the Commission a public presence and report its findings and recommendations to citizens. The site also had an administrative back office where task forces could share preliminary information and communicate online. The site was developed and managed on a server operated by WebTransit, a private provider, to keep the Commission's documents separate from official state business.

In late 2003, staff was added to support the Commission's growing operation. Besides organizing Commission business and communications, it was a full-time job to manage the logistics of task force start-ups, plan meetings and keep work on track for two or three projects in progress.

CNG leadership changed when Bill Todd left to head the Georgia Cancer Coalition. Annie Hunt Burriss moved into the Executive Director's position. Nordholz stayed as deputy. In January 2004, a managing director was appointed as the task force liaison to the Commission, Governor's Office and CNG staff. To reinforce the business partnership on staff, new Managing Director Jerry Guthrie came aboard as an executive-on-loan from BellSouth, where he was Corporate Director for Ethics & Compliance. Guthrie was a University of Georgia business graduate with an MBA in management from Southern Mississippi. Brenda Wise, an organizational whiz who had worked in several state positions, was recruited as project manager. She produced the considerable office support required to run Commission and task force activities. Two college interns were also assigned to the Commission office.

At the beginning of 2004, James Stovall and Katie Beacham joined CNG's Deloitte team on site. The initial task forces were underway, and Deloitte's role turned to making the templates operational and guiding the task force process.

Stovall identified Deloitte's primary objective as lowering barriers that get in the way of the business task, which was to deliver high-quality, usable recommendations to the Governor. He drew it as a simple triangle of meeting needs: "Business wants to help. Government wants their ideas. The Commission is the means."

The first barrier was time. Even with consulting partners, task forces didn't have time to burn on inventing structure and processes. Stovall said Deloitte's organizational groundwork flattened the administrative barrier, so task forces could move ahead in applying their expertise where it mattered most. That was also a help to the task forces' consulting partners – competitors of Deloitte.

"By standardizing processes and lowering the administrative barriers, we made it less expensive for the other consultants to participate so they could focus on the problem, not on the administrative template and process," Stovall said. "Yes, we were working with competitors, but it was smooth. We all saw what we were doing as a benefit to the state."

The Deloitte team attended all meetings in their eight months with the Commission. They scrutinized the task force output for usability, translating private-sector thinking to public-sector realities. Data had to be scrubbed of political considerations and presented as unvarnished fact. Some topics, such as fleet management, fit the metrics of hard data. Others, such as leadership development, involved human capital where the metrics were qualitative. For soft metrics the framework was the goal: What does it look like and how will certain factors affect the outcome.

Waldrop praised the CNG staff for fully engaging in every aspect of the Project Management phase. Their deep understanding of the Governor's philosophy brought purpose and principles to bear on Deloitte's objectives in developing the task force templates. The staff's obvious respect for the volunteers' time, Waldrop said, focused on shifting the ratio of task force effort from project management details to problem-solving.

"Having a consistent process for recruiting, training, organizing and running meetings, and writing reports may sound like an assembly line and not very creative," Nordholz said. "But that allowed the creativity and innovation to happen within the task group, because they didn't have to spend time and energy on the process.

"I had just read Jim Collins' *Built to Last*, and what jumped out is his comment that good organizations are good time-tellers, but great organizations are great clock-builders. I got to be around Joe Rogers and was fascinated talking with him about how Waffle House has everything down to a science. Nothing was left to chance. I wanted to do that with the task force process."

Deloitte wrapped up their work in mid-summer, 2004, after the first task forces had presented their recommendations to the Commission for A New Georgia, Governor Perdue, and the top executives of the State of Georgia. The product exceeded expectations – the measure of "quality" as defined by the Total Quality Management guru Edward Deming.

At the end of their service, Deloitte left the Commission a turn-key project management manual which would guide hundreds of accomplished citizens in the task of making their government more effective, efficient, accountable and customer-focused.

Now the real work of the Commission was ready to go forward.

———

"I'm surprised that people come to this job with no business experience, and I hurt for them, because it is a chief executive role in diverse operations. We've got 85 departments, 100,000 people who do everything from daycare to road building, and you've got to be conversant in the things that matter. You can't micromanage those, but you've got to be focused on results and agree on those results and measure those results and be willing to hold yourselves transparently to those results you've achieved."

SONNY PERDUE, GOVERNOR OF GEORGIA

CHAPTER TWO TAKE AWAY...

Ultimately, over the next seven years, 24 task forces stuck with the original plan, even as composition of the teams began to vary from purely private-sector teams examining business practices, to larger groups with agency participation grappling with streamlining service delivery.

....

The lessons growing out of the inception of the Commission reflect the Governor's original principle of adding value to every undertaking.

....

Investing in a non-profit, legally-constituted corporation ensures freedom from political entanglements and obligations, opening the door for top executives with diverse opinions to participate in the cause of better government.

....

Choosing the right leadership – respected, successful and passionate about quality – builds an organization in that image.

....

Organizational culture is the glue that cements the commitment and the partnership. The value placed on people "showing up" starts with the Governor.

....

Process is primary to a successful effort. Nailing the details in the methodology of task force projects before the team convenes focuses the energy of their expertise on problem-solving, quality research and sound recommendations.

....

Consultants are indispensable. They bring the broadest and deepest experience of research and analysis to the steering committee.

....

Quality is a product of both the integrity and usability of the recommendations.

....

A professional staff in place is a requirement for efficiently maintaining the corporation as well as the progress of the tasks. A hybrid team of private- and public-sector staff members balances the interests of outside thinking and inside understanding.

CHAPTER THREE

BUSINESS-ENGINGEERING IN THE BUREAUCRACY: THE TASK FORCE STRATEGY

The Commission's business-led task forces marched into the thick of business-as-usual in the bureaucracy, taking on entrenched regimens that had resisted repeated reform attempts by previous commissions.

CNG's strategy broke ranks with the conventional methods of past study committees. The idea was to stay nimble within a structured system. Business-led teams – lean, expert and focused – were deployed two or three at a time on 90-day rotations. Task forces performed the forensics on current operations and delivered actionable recommendations. There was no shortcutting on substance. The effort was highly organized to make maximum use of expert resources, working at the speed of business.

A built-in strength of the strategy was the ability to sustain an ongoing plan of work with a rolling agenda of issues.

WORKING AT THE SPEED OF BUSINESS
....

PEELING THE ONION
....

BUILDING A BODY OF WORK
....

THE DYSFUNCTION OF DECENTRALIZATION

"When Governor Perdue established the Commission for a New Georgia, we had no real idea what a tremendous force had been unleashed to drive our work. It was the best thing we could have done to accomplish our mission."

JIM LIENTZ, CHIEF OPERATING OFFICER, STATE OF GEORGIA

The task forces, particularly the first wave, found themselves in a realm of administrative archaeology, examining the underbelly of the bureaucracy and tools extinct in the business world of the 21st Century.

This would have been déjà vu for William Bowdoin, the late businessman who chaired Governor Carl Sanders' 1963 Commission for Efficiency and Improvement. He noted in his book *The Third Force* that "It hardly seems necessary to comment on the penalty paid by any business that attempts to operate in the style of 35 years ago." He went on to say that is precisely what his commission encountered in state government.

"There have been mammoth growth and certain procedural refinements, but the patchwork system of departmental administration remains essentially the same: tacked on, added to and extended."

Forty years later – after the Sanders, Carter and Miller commissions had prescribed and pressed for nearly identical reforms – *Atlanta Journal-Constitution* columnist Jim Wooten was still writing about a state government "that has grown the way country houses used to – one tacked-on addition at a time."

The issues faced by the CNG task forces cut across disparate topics. But according to CNG managing director Jerry Guthrie, they all started with the finding that "There was no common platform for operations across the state."

Guthrie said the task forces were advised at the outset to "Go back to basics… not to assume any semblance of current business practices are going on. They saw the state was way behind the private sector, probably by 20 years. They started at ground zero."

So, as task forces delved into business processes such as procurement, fleet operations, real estate management, personnel administration and technology services, they were all bumping into the same organizational and modernization issues, not only among each other, but ghosts of commissions past. Bowdoin's report on state government in the 1960s could have been written in 2003:

> "The state had left responsibility for these internal functions solely with the agencies it had created to carry out its service programs, and this decentralized pattern had not produced efficient, economical support activities. Instead, it resulted in numerous inefficiencies, wasteful staffings and poor utilization of equipment.
>
> "The state has no information at a central level…there is no updated central inventory of state property… additionally, state agencies have failed to use central purchasing to obtain benefits of volume purchasing. And most regrettably, there is no central agency in either the legislative or executive branch established to give these matters continuing and serious study."

THE RECURRING THEMES of the 1960s, '70s, and '90s, now faced the 21st Century reformers:

- *Overlapping authority.* Multiple agencies managing pieces and parts of the same functional area resulted in conflict, confusion and cracks among policies and operations. A prime example was state property. Several generations of commissions had repeatedly recommended consolidation of all aspects of real estate management under one authority – but in 2003, buildings, lands, leases and construction were still parceled in four separate agencies.

- *Duplication.* Statewide administrative processes were duplicated in the back offices of scores of agencies using different systems and inconsistent policies and procedures. Agency-based software, written for different platforms, created a Bureaucracy of Babel in translating records to state information systems. The state personnel administration had lost control of human resource functions to individual agencies. Improper job and pay classifications were rampant, and employees were subject to inconsistent personnel policies, procedures and standards.

- *Accountability*. Lack of systematic accountability for physical and financial assets was widespread on a broad spectrum, ranging from assignment of state cars to procedures for establishing state bank accounts.

- *Inefficiency*. Agency productivity was fraught with the inefficiency of outmoded practices, apparent unawareness of current industry standards and obsolete technologies. Hand-processing of thousands of paper files and faxes was still standard operating procedure in data-intensive functions. The prime example was procurement, where the private sector had long since converted to e-purchasing and internet bid solicitation. Large purchases took six-to-nine months to contract, and vendor protests regularly caused setbacks and legal costs.

In customer-serving departments, employees and customers alike dealt with the hassle of poorly designed processes. Renewing a driver's license could take a customer two-to-three hours to complete the circuit for a routine clerical transaction. A parent waited months for a child-support order to reach the court. The overhead of inefficiency wasted citizens' time as well as their money.

Business-as-usual was costing the state top dollar. The cost-loss from piecemealed purchasing was staggering in an enterprise that annually spends over $5 billion in contracting goods and services – that's more than a quarter of the total state budget. It wasn't unusual for different agencies to pay, in some cases, twice the price for the same items from the same vendors. Another cost-driver was uncontrolled risk. More than $100 million a year was being spent "by accident" – settling claims for state vehicle collisions, workplace injuries and other liability payouts – which could be significantly reduced by systematic prevention practices.

One of the most serious issues was delivery of technology services essential for functionality of every aspect of government. The telecommunications and computer networks knit together the systems that allowed government to operate as an enterprise. The inability of the state's technology division to meet either current IT standards or local demand forced departments to carve out tech-support units within their own staff, resulting in more duplication, more cost, more incompatibility and less accountability.

The invisibility of customer service as a value of government was endemic. State agencies simply didn't see a "customer" at the receiving end of their internal or external operations.

IN 21ST CENTURY BUSINESS PRACTICE, the operative concept is "shared services," an updated term for "centralization." In yesteryears, centralization was suspect as a tool of concentrated power for public officials. It was becoming clear, however, that anti-centralization was a source of anarchy in the enterprise. Management responsibilities for an $18 billion budget affecting statewide operations were divvied among 100 silos that did not play well together.

The "New Georgia" task forces were plowing "old Georgia" turf, once again being turned for the seeds of reform.

WORKING AT THE SPEED OF BUSINESS

"We needed to get results in real time, not government years. More time is always on the side of status-quo."

BOB HATCHER, COMMISSION CO-CHAIR

The task force strategy – described by the Governor and Commission co-chairs as a "SWAT" operation – was central to the effectiveness of CNG's game plan for reform. Short-term, lean, sharply focused tactical forces of business experts were unleashed to cut through the rampant underbrush of administrative growth and blow past the enemy of time.

"This was not your grandfather's Commission," said Co-chair Bob Hatcher. "We developed strategies to avoid the pitfalls of the previous slower-paced committees that took a year to do their reports and then saw their recommendations passed on to the same agencies whose procedures they were trying to reform.

"We needed to get results in real time, not government years. More time is always on the side of status-quo."

The task force strategy laid out a process of 90-day project timelines. Two-to-three task forces cycled through each quarter and wrapped up a final report to present at the next Commission meeting. New task forces took their places to keep change churning on a quarterly rotation.

Rather than one huge report coming at the end of a study process with a wheelbarrow of recommendations to tackle, the CNG strategy moved reform on a rolling basis of timely initiatives in manageable packages.

The dynamic process also allowed the Commission freedom to rove the landscape of state operations and pursue issues that came up through task force findings, the Governor's Office and agency leaders. It became a vehicle for on-going improvement throughout the Governor's terms.

THE TASK FORCE SYSTEM WAS STRUCTURED AND STAFFED TO MEET ITS PURPOSE. Each task force had four components: 1) the chair and steering committee, 2) a project management team from a major consulting firm, 3) office and resource support from Commission staff, and 4) liaisons representing key players – one member of the Commission and analysts assigned from the Governor's Office of Planning and Budget and the Governor's Policy Office.

TASK FORCE CHAIRS were top-flight, well-known senior executives who had contacts across a gamut of businesses and the influence to press the right people to serve a 90-day stint. The chair had a major hand in forming the Steering Committee, populated by senior business people with field experience.

The chair also took part in advance work with consulting partners, staff and Governor's Office liaisons, prior to convening the first task force meeting. This preparatory session thoroughly briefed the chair on key elements of the task: the Commission's purpose, the issue and objectives, the consultant's preliminary situation analysis, the resource support at their disposal, and the step-by-step agenda for each meeting to keep the project on track and on time.

Donna Hyland, then COO and now CEO of Children's Healthcare, chaired the Receivables Task Force. The task concerned how the government manages and collects delinquent accounts amounting to billions of dollars in unpaid taxes and other funds owed the state. Some accounts were years and even decades old. Hyland described the orientation session, where consulting partners from KPMG put the initial elements of the task on the table.

"The KPMG folks were experts in governmental accounting and finance and were readily available at all times. The KPMG partners educated me on how the government worked in comparison to what I knew from a public sector/large company point of view.

"At the beginning, we sat down and discussed what we feasibly could achieve and what information was needed to start. Based on the early diagnostics, we determined the scope of what we could accomplish and within the timeframe, where we could make the biggest impact. From there we were able to formulate how we could effectively use the time and abilities of the remaining task force personnel.

"We went into our first meeting of the full task force with a strong model."

The leadership skill of the chair was pivotal in negotiating the give-and-take of a strong, diversified committee, comprising experts in private-sector operations, consultants who bridged the public and private operating environments, and government liaisons ultimately responsible for how solutions would be implemented.

"We educated our task force on our mission, core problem and our proposal for objectives," Hyland said. "Once we pitched the idea, if anyone in the group had more expertise and wanted changes or additions, revisions could be made.

"When you have a diverse group, and they don't really know each other well, we needed time for open dialogue. As chair, I tried to make sure everyone in the room was speaking up."

Task force meetings were generally set up for a half-day work session to provide a sufficient block of time for orientation, discussion, idea-generation and even bonding among members. With some participants traveling across the state, longer sessions made more headway with fewer meetings. The meeting logistics and materials were handled by the CNG staff.

Steering Committees were senior-level people who brought experience, who could answer all of the qualitative questions and who knew what to do with all the facts and analysis. They reviewed research, data and issues from their professional perspectives and steered the analysis toward a consensus on realistic conclusions and recommendations. The Committee also was a resource for identifying additional experts in the public and private sectors to inject specific information or assistance.

"We tried to get people who were knowledgeable and leaders in larger corporations who knew the latest practices," said Guthrie. "Senior members would bring in lieutenants to do the analysis. In asking for assistance from corporations, it's rare we were turned down."

Hyland said the Receivables Task Force represented an array of communities, different industries and varying levels of content expertise. "These types of people were able to understand the language and ask the right questions," she said. "The Commission did a great job with helping select the right members."

The Steering Committee members came together for three major meetings during their work quarter. Their agenda was guided by a detailed template for every phase of the task force procedure, from the initiation of the study to the final report. They shaped the scope of the task, postulated a vision for the outcome, suggested data needed to analyze the current situation, helped in developing a set of meaningful findings, and formulated recommendations for transformative measures. Their homework between meetings was to be attentive to incoming information and communications, make contacts and gather intelligence as assigned, and prepare to discuss ideas, direction and issues at the next session.

CONSULTING PARTNERS served as primary investigators, ferreting out data and documentation from inside government as well as national knowledge bases. They conducted interviews and surveys with agency heads and personnel to shape a qualitative dimension of the managerial situation. For the consulting firms, this was a full-time project commitment with a team of at least one experienced consultant and a researcher assigned for the duration of the task force.

"Early task forces had substantial consulting groups which did extensive interviewing," Guthrie said. "They were experienced in working with public sector groups and knew the questions to ask and what data to go after."

An example of an early partner was McKinsey & Company which took on one of the Commission's most complex and comprehensive studies, the state's massive and messy procurement operation. Procurement Task Force Chair Jim Balloun, CEO of Acuity Brands, asked a principal at McKinsey's Atlanta office to consider helping the project with some pro bono work, and got the yes.

The McKinsey team was led by Andy Eversbusch, a young partner experienced in purchasing issues. McKinsey periodically flew in Chip Hardt from Chicago as a special advisor; he had completed a paid project to reform procurement for the State of Illinois, which was realizing substantial savings from its new system. Amy Mulkey, a junior staffer (and reigning Miss Georgia), was assigned as fulltime researcher. Eversbusch, who has since moved to another firm, said McKinsey treated the pro bono project with no less commitment than any paying customer would receive.

> "One of the lessons for government is to be sure the company that engages in the pro bono work, as many do, is giving full effort to the study. The consultant should bring the same rigor and structure to the project as with any client, which McKinsey did. There is a big price to be paid if it is not good work, or the information is not sound. It was fundamental to do it right, rather than sprinkling expertise in here and there or making high-level recommendations. From the McKinsey side, a lot of elements were put in place to make this a robust project."

Eversbusch and Mulkey interviewed more than 30 "stakeholders" in state government, both within the procurement department and the customer it served in other agencies. The research entailed combing through the fragmented functions scattered across the procurement organization, tracing the process to pitfalls, drilling data that had never been collected before, and analyzing systems, practices and tools. The team also drew on a broad research base of practices in the field, as well as experience with other public and private procurement projects.

With guidance, review and input from the Steering members, Eversbusch produced the final report to the Commission. It ran 70 pages, including nearly 40 charts of findings, data, process flow, and supporting analysis for recommending transformation to a centralized procurement system. Balloun said the contribution of the consultants, from legwork to analysis, was indispensible.

> "It's a great myth that consultants bring in these junior young people who tell you what to do. What the junior people bring in is the ability to find the fact or do the homework it requires to get the solutions. What the more senior people bring is pattern recognition. They've seen this before and have a nose for where the real issues are. A guy like Chip Hardt had literally just gone through it in Illinois."

The work and findings of the procurement task force is a story in itself, to be told later in this book, but McKinsey's experience was repeated by more than a dozen firms of that stature. Each made the same all-out commitment of hundreds of staff hours worth hundreds of thousands of dollars. IBM, Hewitt and Deloitte each did two task forces.

INTERNAL SUPPORT by the Commission staff covered the logistics of setting up the task force meetings, opening doors for interviews with agency heads, staff and other officials, and facilitating access to government information. Liaisons from the Office of Planning and Budget knew the performance and fiscal history within functional areas. Representatives of the Governor's policy staff reviewed output and kept the executive chiefs apprised.

From a consultant's perspective, Eversbusch said, the right strengths were lined up to run an effective task force:

- Sponsorship from the private sector is a substantial asset. The Procurement Task Force, for example, was represented by chief purchasing officers from companies the caliber of Home Depot and Coca-Cola.

  "People like this brought a level of experience and credentials that added credibility to the report," Eversbusch said. "Their role in reviewing the material put their leadership experience behind recommendations. They did the reality check: 'Does this make sense?'"

- The right task force chair is pivotal in the exercise of leadership and "the pull to bring a lot of expertise to the table."

- The governor and his lieutenants are fully on board, indicating the chain of command was in place for implementing recommendations.

"In some pro bono projects there's a big question whether this will lead to a meaningful impact," said Eversbusch. "This whole set-up worked very well. Heads of each department took it seriously and took time. They recognized it as an earnest effort to improve."

AGENCY OFFICIALS might have been expected to take on a defensive posture. By and large, they didn't. CNG Deputy Director Kris Nordholz helped arrange interviews and fact-seeking sessions between consultants and the agencies they were scrutinizing.

"When we first started, we had a new Governor from a party none of these agency heads had worked under," Nordholz said. "There was a lot of unease among those who had been in state government a long time and wondered what would happen, especially as the Commission task forces started snooping around their areas. But no one stonewalled. They wanted to understand what we were doing and wanted to help."

As a task force chair, Hyland deliberately solicited agency input as smart strategy:

> "We asked the consultants to interview each of the agency heads for their opinions on what we should do. We knew they had answers and could pinpoint the weak areas. They had a lot of great ideas which helped us formulate our plan. Many times, they knew there was a better way to do things, but ran into restrictions because of how government is operated.

> "We were able to foster their acceptance by bringing forward some of their recommendations, which maybe they had been trying to do themselves. That is common with any business; the people on the front lines are usually the ones with the best ideas. The process was very collaborative. People immediately gelled around the idea of how can we make this better."

Commission member Swearingen, who served as liaison to the Customer Service Task Force, said he learned over time that the findings and recommendations for reform were rarely a shock to agency insiders. "Government folks had thought about it, read about it, or even tried it, but they did not have the political cover or the resources available to make the move. The Commission became an important catalyst for saying that new thoughts, ideas, new ways of doing business are open."

TASK FORCE MEMBERS BROUGHT THE VALUE-ADDED ADVANTAGE of exposure to multiple environments, business organizations and challenges, Swearingen said. "They didn't have tunnel vision focused on only a finite set of questions or issues, but they were given the opportunity to bring their thoughts and ideas to the table, which became actions to be implemented."

Hyland said that was the case for the Receivables Task Force, which started out looking at delinquent accounts and happened upon a surprising find: State agencies had opened an estimated 2,000 individual bank accounts,

TASK FORCE EVALUATIONS: NOTHING PERSONAL

It is important to note that agency leaders and personnel were not evaluated by consultants or task forces on their professional knowledge, skill or fitness for the function they operated. Task forces confined observations to operational outcomes. Nevertheless, one of the conundrums for task forces was keeping the nuts-and-bolts issues separated from the competence of the people involved.

In Georgia, as in any bureaucracy, department heads include a sizeable contingent of long-time state employees who move up the ranks, some from agency to agency, as they are promoted on their seniority and success in the system. While management experience in government is valuable, it isn't necessarily tuned-in to areas where knowledge of current industry practices would be critical to effectiveness. The learning curve in complex, high-maintenance functions like procurement and personnel administration is steep; some commissioners "didn't know what they didn't know" about the area they were administering. Departments also tended to be staffed by employees hired to do a job as it is put in front of them, in the way it has "always been done." Bureaucracy is rarely a fertile environment for innovation, initiative and improvement.

The Perdue Administration was marked by high turnover in agency leadership. CNG recommendations precipitated some change at the top, by pointing to reforms that called for management-level insight and skill sets typically honed by experience in the profession.

Throughout the Perdue years, there has been a growing presence of agency and authority commissioners new to state government, coming in with private-sector experience and credentials from the field they were administering. These pros had the skills to turn the curve to new business methods on a faster track.

That said, a cadre of high-profile lifers in state government leadership also stayed with the Governor's program. These were seasoned leaders who embraced the new culture and even postponed retirement to become agents of change.

accruing thousands of dollars in service charges, while returning minimal interest. In some departments, bank deposits were made when it was convenient. Checks might be squirreled in desk drawers for days or weeks, while they could have been in the bank earning interest. In many cases, accounts were unaudited. The anomaly was picked up through many sets of eyes scrutinizing information, Hyland said.

"Each person had such a diverse background. For example, David Hanna was president of CommuCredit which processes credit cards, but he also had a background in finance. A lot of great ideas came out of the group. We prioritized the three or four things we were going to focus on, but then as we got other ideas, we cataloged those. In our report we were able to say, here are specific recommendations on these three or four priority areas, but we also gave a laundry list of other ideas."

One of the spinoffs of the Receivables Task Force was streamlined banking, the consolidation of dozens of small accounts into higher-interest funds with regulated practices. Leadership for the streamlining initiative came through Georgia's first State Accounting Office, established by recommendation of the Receivables Task Force. The number of accounts was eventually pared to about 400. Although the number is exponentially higher than a corporate enterprise would tolerate, it offered a satisfactory solution for legislators who believed in sharing state holdings among banks in their districts.

Compromise is bound to happen in government, but "the value of the business-led task force," Guthrie said, "was to see things in a different light, with no entanglements to the agencies and functions being reviewed. They still operate within those parameters."

PEELING THE ONION

"Peeling back the onion was the real essence of the task forces when they got into a subject. Go back and look at task forces that stemmed from another. Risk management is a good example. No one wanted to include that on our list until the issue came up in fleet management."

CARL SWEARINGEN, COMMISSION MEMBER

The selection of CNG's first-year task force topics spearheaded a spectrum of new directions that the administration wanted to take in asset management, leadership and customer service, and in developing a state business plan for economic growth. The parameters stretched as the value of business assessment became apparent in a variety of areas which could improve their performance with a management make-over.

As task forces began to drill, they sometimes struck a pocket of deviance from business standards, such as the mushrooming bank accounts. These matters were beyond the carefully defined scope of the task force mission, but needed to get on the executive branch's radar. As corollary issues came up, the Commission had the freedom to convene new task forces to carry on with the sequel.

So, as the onion gave up its layers, were the revelations worse than expected? Swearingen's answer: "Let's say the opportunities were more."

"Property was a good example. We knew we had no list of our buildings. This was a basic high-level issue. But once you started peeling back into that, you also see the construction manual hasn't been updated since 1950. Nobody would have known that at the beginning, but look how important that has been when you're investing a billion dollars every year into new construction."

When Georgia's first State Property Officer was established as a result of Commission recommendations, the new SPO's to-do list included the Governor's personal order to create a uniform contracting and construction manual. The new state manual is now online, guiding the on-time, on-budget progress of capital projects through end-to-end uniform procedures and practices. Construction firms had been begging for this breakthrough for decades.

THE DYNAMIC OF SPINNING-OFF OF PROJECTS, whether with a whole new task force or a follow-up action by the Governor's Office, has been a core strength of the Commission's creation as a living, breathing organization capable of responding to opportunity.

Particularly in the Governor's second term, topics surfaced from situations where the resources of the Commission could be brought to bear in comprehending the business side of a major operation or policy thrust – for example, public works programs.

"Significant issues that were policy-related tended to deal with behind-the-scenes areas that would help larger committees get goals accomplished," Guthrie said. He cited transportation and freight and logistics as examples.

Transportation was a thorn in every governor's backside – the cost, the highway hassles, the orange barrels that went on for miles and years. On a national scale, Metro Atlanta was commuter hell. Perdue wanted a CNG task force to analyze cost-drivers in contracting and managing highway construction projects. He wanted to determine whether the state was getting bang for the buck in its $2 billion investment in his Fast Forward plan. This was a monumental concern as the state headed into comprehensive strategic planning for a multi-modal, multi-billion dollar system.

The 2007 CNG Transportation Task Force was chaired by Commission member Neal Purcell, retired Partner of KPMG and vice chairman of its national audit operations. Deloitte provided the consulting firepower with a team of three executive- and management-level analysts. The task force earned the distinction of presenting the longest report in CNG history – 86 pages of forensics on three primary business concerns: market factors affecting competitive bids and cost of materials; government barriers to efficient spending strategies and project delivery; and opportunities to streamline highway project management.

The task force also put Georgia's spending data up against other states to compare trend lines in what highway money was buying. The task force showed Georgia channeling the lion's share of funds into resurfacing and maintaining highways. Meanwhile, other states spent more increasing capacity, "adding lanes" to address congestion. The assessment streamed data into the statewide planning process to inform priority-setting.

The transportation report spawned a sequel task force the next year on the freight and logistics industry as a strategic component of transportation planning, as well as an economic driver. The task force, for the first time, traced all the intermodal forms of freight movement to and through Georgia's transportation infrastructure, marking potential hubs for growth of distribution centers and related businesses.

As the task forces clearly brought sophisticated resources to business analysis, CNG's reach expanded into current issues: marketing intellectual property created by Georgia's research universities to draw new business to the state; liberalizing the investment strategies of state pension funds for greater growth;

and adjusting cost and quality in employee health benefits to contain the state's subsidy and liability.

These task force reports became the business case in a stunning array of transformation initiatives.

BUILDING A BODY OF WORK

"We had task forces on the things that we think contribute to a best-managed company or a state, giving value to its shareholders or its citizens. This has been in place since I came into office in 2003, so we'll have a seven-and-a-half-year run of best-managed practices for our state, driven by best practices of business and processes."

GOVERNOR SONNY PERDUE, 2008 PEW TRUST PANEL ON MANAGING GOVERNMENT

The first wave of four task forces started wading into assigned areas beginning in September and October 2003. The lineup was Space Management, Capital Construction, Leadership Development, and Tourism. The 24th and last task force reported January 2009 on state investment strategies for pension funds.

When possible, Governor Perdue attended the task force launch meeting. The experience of sitting around the conference table with the Governor of the State saying "I'm counting on you" delivered a powerful message about the task and inspired effort for excellent work. He closed with a caveat: "Be careful what you recommend, because it will be implemented in your state." For members, it became a personal act of citizenship.

Built into each final report meeting, prior to the formal presentation at the quarterly CNG session, was a tête-à-tête among the task force chair, CNG liaison, key staff and the Governor himself. The purpose was a dry-run through the findings and recommendations so the Governor would be fully informed of all aspects of the situation and solution. Politics were rarely a sticking point, unless there was concern about "do-ability" tied to funding, legislation, or local and vocal interest reaction.

"From everything I have seen, this Governor has relied on his team, is interested in ideas, and even though he has his own opinions, he is willing to listen to other people's thoughts and ideas," said Swearingen, who attended numerous preview sessions.

"His looking for something else did not change his willingness to look at what he got. In most cases, the task forces, consultants and CNG leadership were left alone. I don't ever recall someone saying, 'You are going to look at customer service, but this is how I want you to do it.' We appreciated it more as suggestions, as in, 'Here are three little off-sets you might want to pursue,' which produced recommendations 10, 11 and 12."

THE TASK FORCE'S FINAL PRESENTATION to the distinguished body of Commission members in the Governor's Mansion had the aura of a special event. Task force chairs presented well-crafted PowerPoints on a projection screen. The reports were thorough but brief, typically with the following content:

- Summary of the problem or issue of the present situation and its consequences
- Findings and business analysis from the study
- Options for solutions with pros and cons
- Recommended actions
- The cost, requirements and potential barriers to implementation
- Next steps to accomplish implementation

The slide presentations were supplemented with detailed hard-copy reports. At the session, the task force chairs fielded the Q&A, followed by the Governor's comments.

After the Commission meeting, the task force summaries and final reports were posted on their website www.newgeorgia.org for public consumption. The site was a repository for all task force reports and recommendations, and maintained an up-to-date scorecard for implementation actions.

FROM WHERE THE COMMISSION MEMBERS SAT, it was clear that a body of work was building on a scheduled basis to position the executive branch for action, backed by credible recommendations. The quarterly reporting sustained momentum. This in itself was modeling a "new way of doing business" in government – with deliberate speed and an expectation for action.

In 2004, when task force recommendations began transitioning to the implementation phase, the quarterly CNG meetings served a triple purpose: 1) launching new initiatives, 2) receiving reports and recommendations from completed task forces, and 3) tracking progress of recommended actions being put to work inside government.

CNG charter member John Rice is Vice Chairman of General Electric and President and Chief Executive Officer of GE Infrastructure. In his estimation, the Commission proved itself "a worthwhile effort for everyone who has been a part of it."

"I think there were probably Commission members who wanted to wait to see if the Governor was really serious. You never know when you start out in something like this whether this is going to be an idea that never materializes into anything. Are people going to get bored, are commitments going to wane, will the Governor delegate it to somebody? None of that happened."

Rice saw prudence in the pace of change proceeding with planned steps. "In every situation I am aware of, with respect to the Commission, there was a bias for action with caution where necessary."

As managing director, Guthrie negotiated incoming task force projects and said the Commission unfailingly embraced the requests that came their way. "To their credit, the Commission was not about flashy things," Guthrie said. "They were about making government better and getting down to the things that just needed to be done. These were primarily internal."

As new topics were added to the task force list, the membership broadened to include expertise from academia, governmental management associations, and consultants from the University System's institutes of government and economic development. Larger, hybrid task forces which impacted delivery of public services brought agency officials into the loop as members.

In the six years from 2003 to 2009 that the Commission was actively launching task forces, 260 citizens from more than 50 Georgia cities, and 64 consultants from 21 premier firms were enlisted to serve. The 24 task forces generated 130 recommendations.

The list of task forces illustrates the breadth and diversity of the areas of government impacted by astute, actionable recommendations.

COMMISSION TASK FORCES

ENTERPRISE MANAGEMENT
→ ADMINISTRATIVE SERVICES
→ PROCUREMENT

ASSET MANAGEMENT
→ FLEET (2 TASK FORCES)
→ AVIATION

REAL ESTATE
→ SPACE MANAGEMENT
→ CAPITAL CONSTRUCTION

FINANCIAL MANAGEMENT
→ RECEIVABLES
→ PUBLIC FINANCE OPTIONS
→ STATE INVESTMENT STRATEGIES

COST MANAGEMENT
→ RISK MANAGEMENT
→ STATE HEALTH BENEFITS

CULTURE OF STEWARDSHIP AND SERVICE
→ LEADERSHIP DEVELOPMENT
→ CUSTOMER SERVICE
→ RECRUITMENT-RETENTION-RETIREMENT OF STATE EMPLOYEES

SERVICE DELIVERY
→ SERVICE DELIVERY
→ COMMUNITY CARE FOR BEHAVIORAL HEALTH AND
   DEVELOPMENTAL DISORDERS

ECONOMIC GROWTH
→ WORKFORCE DEVELOPMENT
→ STRATEGIC INDUSTRIES
→ COMPETITIVENESS
→ INTELLECTUAL PROPERTY/COMMERCIALIZATION
→ FREIGHT AND LOGISTICS
→ TRANSPORTATION

THE DYSFUNCTION OF DECENTRALIZATION

"The four primary administrative agencies of the State* have overlapping responsibilities for policy making, in some cases are not fulfilling their chartered responsibility, and overall lack the governance structure to effectively and efficiently provide administrative services to other State agencies."

TASK FORCE ON ADMINISTRATIVE SERVICES REPORT, APRIL 13, 2004

In the first year, task forces were primarily grappling with the disorder created by decentralization in asset management, human resources and technology. The Administrative Services Task Force identified this as a common snafu in government operations.

The quote above was the first bullet in the task force's summary, followed by four specific issues:

- The current organizational structure wasn't achieving effective accountability.

- The operating cost of the services for the four agencies was $400 million, which was buying limited service with a poor reputation for quality.

- Technology was being under-utilized for effective and efficient administrative services.

- Key leadership skill gaps existed in each agency, impacting their effectiveness.

The Administrative Services Task Force was chaired by Jim Copeland, retired CEO of Deloitte Touche. He had led the firm though its greatest period of growth to become the second-largest professional services organization in the world.

The task force charge was to evaluate the effectiveness and efficiency of the State's administrative operations in terms of agency core missions and recommend a best-practice methodology to improve operations. Areas of focus included governance, accountability, organization and key business process activities. Options for improvement included privatization, consolidation and streamlining opportunities.

The good news, according to the task force, was that "many opportunities exist to consolidate the administrative functions residing in the four agencies

*The agencies were Department of Administrative Services, the Georgia Building Authority, the Georgia Technology Authority and the Georgia Merit System.

to improve accountability and service delivery."

The business-sector group made a pointed observation about government and the necessity to impose formal measures for accountability:

> "The private sector can rely on the marketplace to gauge its performance but public entities have no such indicator. Therefore, a proxy must be created to assist in the measurement of service delivery success. The State should institute a standards-and-measures function to assist with the development of meaningful measures by which to judge performance, and also provide validation to the level of success achieved."

In its initial evaluation, the task force cited the "industry best practices" benchmark for "operational excellence" as an eight-to-ten percent improvement in efficiency a year. They looked at the current state as a gauge of the gains to be made. Quoting from the report:

> We spend greater than…
>
> …$400 million annually for government-to-government services…which has a fragmented governance structure and a poor reputation for service.
>
> …$4 billion annually to procure goods and services with limited visibility to maximize purchasing power.
>
> …$15 million more annually for HR functions than we did 8 years ago.
>
> …$400 million annually on information technology with a limited capability to manage and monitor the effectiveness of the investment.
>
> …$14 billion in owned assets with fragmented stewardship.

By these figures, the projected cost savings for meeting operational efficiency standards exceeded $700 million a year.

The task force identified areas of overlap and conflict in governance of real estate management, fleet management and procurement of technology products and services, as well as critical fragmentation in personnel administration. All of these topics were dealt with in detail by later task forces, but the Administrative Services report presented a clear overview of basic flaws across the spectrum of internal, enterprise-level services.

The task force also drafted a blueprint for shared services. It aligned core administrative functions within agencies by mission to "promote clear policy-making authority and enforcement, defined accountability and customer-focused operations." The new organization at the enterprise level looked like this:

- An expanded Administrative Services division for asset management, procurement and common services.
- A cohesive Personnel Administration over all human capital development and management programs and employee benefits.
- A Technology Authority for IT value-management of policy, planning and projects and responsibility for products and services.
- A Financial Division encompassing money management, planning and budget, investments, and payroll.

In each area, the task force detailed the estimated costs and savings of moving to new organizational orders, the metrics and performance benefits, the estimated time frame for the transformation, as well as the risks and barriers to making the changes.

THE ITEMIZATION OF BARRIERS TO TRANSFORMATION under each functional area was instructive in understanding how the ruling culture of government interfered with instituting effective management. Here are excerpts from the various lists:

- Legislation which had originated the separation of related functions into different agencies.
- The questionable inclination and ability of agencies to get on board with change.
- Retaining the flexibility of authorities to manage assets.
- Agency dissatisfaction with poor services in IT and procurement and lack of trust in centralizing those responsibilities.
- Reluctance of agencies to relinquish control of personnel management.
- Lack of skill and leadership in existing functions.
- The short-term cost of investing to upgrade technologies.
- Legislation required to reorganize.
- No teeth in compliance and enforcement of policy.
- Lack of integrated systems for management.

Summarizing a 72-page report leaves out more than it covers. Much that is missing in this brief account shows up in later task force studies which took on the thorniest areas as transformation projects.

As with all task forces, the Administrative Services report left several tips for follow-up. One would come back as a potential deal-breaker between the executive-driven administrative advances and the legislative-controlled budget process:

> "Budget Reform – New budget practices should be considered to reward savings. The current use-or-lose budget practices do not reward savings, but actually penalize savings initiatives. Adoption of new practices will not only allow departments to be better stewards of their State funds and provide better services to their customers, but also will allow the State to more effectively interact with a private sector that is becoming ever more competitive and demand driven."

———

"I challenged task forces to be working partners in re-engineering Georgia's bureaucratic machinery into a 21ˢᵗ Century business model. They were being asked to do more than help state agencies work through a task list of tactical problems. Their charge was to initiate a management turnaround: converting bureaucracy-as-usual to business principles and best practices across the board in government. In short, to transform Georgia to the best-managed state in America, giving the best value citizens can get anywhere in the public sector."

SONNY PERDUE, GOVERNOR OF GEORGIA

CHAPTER THREE TAKE AWAY...

TASK FORCES AT THEIR BEST ARE...

Diversified in relevant expertise

....

Led by a strong, collegial executive oriented to the task

....

Clearly defined by scope, objectives and end date

....

Structured to take full advantage of focused time and substantive information

....

Supported by resources of a sharp, organized staff

....

Embedded with staff in executive chain-of-command

STRATEGIES THAT WORK FOR RESULTS ARE...

Serial task forces, rotating on short (quarterly) cycles, to produce timely recommendations in a manageable sequence

....

Leadership attention and appreciation at the highest level for the work of the participants

....

A formal presentation of the final report in front of the Governor and Commission

....

Public access to reports and recommendations

SUSTAINABILITY IS FOSTERED AT THE COMMISSION LEVEL BY...

Pursuing spinoff issues in sequel task forces

....

Openness to opportunities for taking both leading and supporting roles in working through important issues

....

Stretching the parameters of the "business" of state government to include the financial and management aspect of major program and planning challenges

MAKING CHANGE REALLY HAPPEN: THE IMPLEMENTATION IMPERATIVE

A year into the Commission's work, the Administration was at a point where the impetus of transformation could have turned to inertia. Thirty recommendations had accumulated on the Governor's desk. Now what?

This was the slippery slope where previous commissions' recommendations didn't get traction where the rubber meets the road – inside the bureaucracy.

Governor Perdue made good on his pledge to be held accountable for results. He appointed a Director of Implementation, whose singular job was to put innovation into operation using all resources on deck, backed 100 percent by the executive team.

Contrary to popular notions about bureaucratic behavior, administrators stepped up as champions of change. Many had been waiting years for their voices to be heard.

THE NATIONAL CHAMPIONSHIP OF GOOD GOVERNMENT

TEAM GEORGIA

GAME PLAN

GROUND GAME

EXECUTION

WHOSE BALL?

NO TIMEOUTS

"If you had to weigh the order on a set of scales, the task force effort and the implementation effort would weigh the same. If you had to unbalance it, you'd rather have less out of the task forces and more out of implementation, because that's what lasts."

JOE ROGERS, COMMISSION CO-CHAIR

May 26, 2004. One year, almost to the day, since Governor Sonny Perdue had announced the chartering of the Commission for A New Georgia, a core group of 15 leaders and lieutenants of the Administration, the Office of Planning and Budget, and the Commission held a retreat at the Governor's Mansion to decide the next steps. By then, more than two dozen recommendations were on Perdue's desk waiting for something to happen.

As Commission Co-chair Bob Hatcher put it, "Some of the folks in state government thought they were drinking from a fire hose, so much stuff was coming out for them to implement."

The initial six task forces had started in Fall 2003 and reported to the Commission in the first and second quarters of 2004. Their recommendations called for momentous changes in the business and culture of major areas of government. The Governor's leadership team, policy deputies, budget analysts and Commission staff were contemplating a follow-up strategy. The deciders were assembled that day to come up with a plan.

The pivotal question was, "Who owns the implementation process?"

"If you simply delegate the results of these task forces to department heads, you'll be frustrated," CNG Co-chair Joe Rogers told the gathering. "We're getting some really useful stuff from the task forces. If you want it done, you've got to have a champion. Jim (Lientz, Chief Operating Officer) is too bogged down and overloaded with what he's got to do in the organization."

A number of options were up for review – from hiring a consulting firm to manage the process and projects, to making the Office of Planning and Budget (OPB) the point agency.

The earliest straw man was the OPB model. In this scenario, the agency would appoint a working group for each project, with the objective to translate and transition CNG recommendations into transformation measures. OPB's guardian angel would be the Governor's Implementation Steering Committee (GISC). The committee would comprise the chief operating and financial officers and their deputies, the director and deputy of OPB, plus CNG staff. They would meet every other week.

It was a mini-model of classic bureaucracy – incorporating all the elements of failed plans of previous post-commission efforts. Implementation would be reduced to a tacked-on responsibility for an existing agency attempting to direct actions within peer agencies. Executive decisions would be made by committee. Responsibility and authority for monitoring progress and outcomes would be diffused among OPB, the leadership team and agencies. That's how everybody's job becomes nobody's job.

It was the first and favored of five options presented at the retreat:

1. Activate the OPB-owner model, using internal state resources, with the sponsorship of the chief operating and financial officers.

2. Engage two-to-three outside individuals, possibly retired executives, who were seasoned in implementation and change-management. The cost was estimated at $250-500,000.

3. Hire a consulting firm to set up and operate a Program Management Office and change-management activities. The approximate cost would be in the $1 million range for management assistance and up to $10 million to run the full operation for several years.

4. Combine #2 and the less-comprehensive version of #3 at an approximate cost of $1.5 million.

5. Bring in a leader for each implementation area on a two-to-three year stint, looking to the private sector for loaned executives.

A daunting mission faced any of the above. At the retreat, participants considered a list of potential barriers to implementation. The last item was "historical inability to effect change." At the bottom line, that was the challenge.

Any form of an implementation program would start at square one and face an organizational obstacle course of hurdles and hoops:

- Uncertainty about the continuing commitment of funding resources, support staff and senior-level sponsorship

- Possible resistance from legislators to reassigning administrative control of functions designated by legislation

- Policy or structural constraints to instituting enterprise-level administration

- Pushback by agency heads and employees

- Absence of an existing centralized management structure or formal management processes to be the platform for implementing major changes

The way forward needed a light at the end of the tunnel, and that light was to be the shining example of a "best-managed state."

THE NATIONAL CHAMPIONSHIP OF GOOD GOVERNMENT

"Best-Managed State only means something to policy wonks. What we are trying to tell the public is that good management means good value. Best-Managed State was the effort to try to 'brand' the process. It evolved into the things we were trying to do."

GOVERNOR SONNY PERDUE

Commission recommendations were clearly pressing the Governor to adopt centralized management of cross-government functions and "shared services" at the enterprise level as the business model for a "best-managed state."

On the retreat agenda, the question for decision was, "Does Georgia want to make this an enterprise-level effort?" Equally important was the corollary, "Will agency-level leadership be held accountable by the Governor or COO/CFO?"

There was no ambiguity in Perdue's affirmation. "Obviously, implementing so many recommendations involving a variety of agencies is going to be a difficult and time-consuming process. But I want everyone to understand that this is a top priority of mine."

The first piece was already in place. The Administration's top-level organization chart ran reporting lines from agencies to the COO or CFO, who created an all-points communication channel via weekly meetings. This forged the critical chain of accountability.

The quest to become Best-Managed State was more than a slogan. It was the drive to win the national championship of good government.

Commission recommendations carried the imprimatur of impeccably qualified business leaders and world-class consulting firms. But even better, they dovetailed neatly with the criteria which the Pew Center for the States applies in its triennial Government Performance Project (GPP). The next GPP survey was about to start in June 2004, and grades would be announced in the February 2005 issue of *Governing*. The ranking was popularly known as "America's Best-Managed States." Georgia's 2001 grade of B-minus fell in the middle of the average tier.

The GPP criteria provided a framework for performance in four management areas where CNG was addressing specific shortcomings:

- *Money*. Managing fiscal resources, including budgeting, forecasting, accounting and financial reporting, procurement, contracting, investing, and debt management.

- *People*. Managing employees, including creating an effective and efficient system for hiring, retention and rewards, and planning for leadership succession.

- *Infrastructure*. Managing physical infrastructure, including roads, bridges, buildings, information technology systems, and other resources supported by capital expenditures.

- *Information*. Using information and technology to measure the effectiveness of services, communicate with citizens, and help managers and elected leaders make good decisions.

Within these four categories were 77 points of conformance with best practices. It formed a checklist for states to stack up their strengths and weaknesses against national benchmarks.

"At the time we took office, our quest to make Georgia the best-managed state in the nation sounded either audacious or ridiculous," said COO

Jim Lientz. "Our driver's license lines were broken; we weren't delivering services well; we couldn't get our financial audits out on time; and we'd suffered back-to-back revenue declines for the first time since the Great Depression."

Chief of Staff John Watson said Perdue's goal to rank Georgia among the best-managed states "put a marker out there for measuring success and focus on what we should be doing well. It was also a way of keeping the Commission on its main task rather than straying into policy and legislative issues."

The discipline of benchmarking created that "cycle of accountability" which Lientz said is a strong suit of business and a shortcoming of government.

"Along the way, our aspiration to become the best-managed state created focus for us," Lientz said. "I came from an environment where we had to report earnings quarterly. This can be exhilarating or humiliating, but it absolutely creates focus. I quickly saw that government had no deadlines like that, and we have used conversations about the progress we are making in the performance criteria to help us create the required focus.

"The goal of being a best-managed state by 2007 captivated imagination, challenged us to actually try to accomplish this, and kept it going by knowing the evaluation was going to happen on a periodic basis."

The Commission also focused on the best-managed challenge as a motivating factor for their mission, said Carl Swearingen, who represented the board at the retreat.

"It gave us the target," he said. "This is all about winning the game. You can have your best quarterback or kicker – in our case strategic planning or property management – but did you win the game? The best-managed state says you are trying to win the game. It forced us to address the outcome of all of these improvements."

At the end of the day, the group had agreement on the responsibility of the Governor and executive leadership team to hold agencies accountable for implementation. They also got a reality check on the Administration's readiness to implement big, complex projects with the present resources and culture. There was a formidable list of prerequisites in notes from the retreat.

The plan at that point was to regroup, settle on an implementation "owner," and be prepared to bring it to the Commission's quarterly meeting July 13, a month-and-a-half away.

REALITY CHECKLIST

GOVERNANCE
- Establish an enterprise-level governance team

PROJECT MANAGEMENT
- Create initiative scorecards to track progress
- Create a centralized project management office
- Create budget and savings management structure
- Create baselines upon which to measure success
- Develop criteria to prioritize initiatives
- Prioritize current initiatives and get started
- Develop detailed initiative business cases
- Create model for agency vs. enterprise benefits

COMMUNICATIONS
- Identify and analyze key stakeholders (by initiative and overall)
- Create marketing campaign to constituents
- Create marketing campaign to state staff
- Create a website for constituents and staff
- Create legislative briefing documents

SPONSORSHIP
- Governor proclamation of an Enterprise Program
- Agency Head announcement of support for program
- Obtain Legislative buy-in

RESOURCES
- Secure funding to support initiatives
- Hire staff for centralized project management effort
- Define roles and responsibilities of state and potential contractors to support initiatives; estimate resource requirements

CULTURE AND CONSENSUS
- Assess cultural barriers of key stakeholders
- Initiatives or enterprise program
- Engage state employees through initiative identification programs
- Assess recommendations by key stakeholders

TEAM GEORGIA

"I was told I would be responsible for coming to work every day and dealing with everything it took to make this happen. It turned out that I would eat, sleep and live implementation."

LONICE BARRETT, DIRECTOR, GOVERNOR'S OFFICE OF IMPLEMENTATION

The Commission was one of those proverbial "best-kept secrets" in state government. Awareness was mostly confined to agencies where the initial task force consultants came knocking.

Lonice Barrett, Commissioner of the Department of Natural Resources, hadn't heard of CNG until he got a call after the retreat from Executive Director Annie Hunt Burriss, inquiring what he knew about the Commission. "Really, not a thing," he told her.

Soon after came a call from COO Jim Lientz on behalf of the Governor, wanting to talk about a proposition. Barrett and Lientz were both readying to head to duty posts at Sea Island, where the 2004 G-8 Conference was being hosted by President Bush starting June 8. They agreed to meet in Savannah and ride to Brunswick together to explore a deal.

"Jim said the Governor had expressed interest in my taking the job of implementing significant changes in the way state government was doing business," Barrett recalls. "Ironically, I had just made up my mind to retire after the 2005 legislative session."

Barrett had over 30 years service in state government, the last decade as DNR Commissioner. His name had initially surfaced at the May retreat as the ideal candidate for a possible implementation champion. Barrett was an insider who was trusted, seasoned and often introduced as "the hardest working man in state government." He had more friends in the General Assembly than any state administrator and went out of his way to know his fellow agency heads. Despite retirement plans, he was drawn to the challenge as a capstone of his lifelong service to Georgia and out of his personal respect for Sonny Perdue. "I would not have ever postponed retirement for anyone except Governor Perdue," he said.

Barrett asked about reporting directly to the Governor. He saw the leverage as essential to enlisting the right people to implement projects across agencies. Perdue concurred, and on July 22 announced the appointment.

"Commissioner Barrett has proven himself to be one of our most respected and effective state administrators in solving problems, controlling costs and improving service in his agency," the Governor said. "I am asking him to apply his leadership and experience to transforming the culture of state government across the board. He's the perfect person to implement the Commission's constructive findings and creative solutions."

The same week, unrelated to his appointment, Barrett was featured on the cover of *Georgia Trend* as "the most trusted public servant in state government."

Barrett spent about 16 months as director and lived by his reputation as the "git'er done" guy in government. He had a granite desk plate made, inscribed with the motto "Smart Government Saves and Serves." He saw that as his job, carved in stone.

GAME PLAN

"The perception out there among citizens was that state government could and should be doing better. I had huge hopes and aspirations that we were getting ahead of the curve, before there was an emergency. We were focused on the fact that the state needs to be doing these things as preventive maintenance."
LONICE BARRETT, DIRECTOR, GOVERNOR'S OFFICE OF IMPLEMENTATION

Barrett picked up the voluminous notebook of the first six Commission reports and a blank check to recruit inter-agency implementation teams. Once assembled, the teams were given just over a month to vet the task force blueprints and deliver detailed plans and options to engineer implementation of the recommendations. Their reports would form the project plan. Barrett would become the foreman on the projects, coordinating the executive, policy, agency and legislative actions for the construction-and-operations phase of implementation. He set a deadline to draft executive orders, bills and budget requests ready for pre-legislative politicking in December.

Four implementation teams were formed to tackle the six CNG task force reports, with two teams pairing up related areas. The first round involved a total of more than 60 team members from 26 agencies. Three teams covered high-priority proposals for centralized operations in administrative services and procurement, in space management and capital construction, and in fleet management. The fourth team focused on public/private approaches to boost the economic impact of the state's number one industry, tourism.

Team chairs were selected for knowledge of the area and enthusiasm for the change agenda. The members represented agencies with skin in the game. Everyone involved recognized the stakes: that business-as-usual would be substantively transformed, and their input would determine how to make change work for the best result.

Barrett arranged for each implementation team to meet with the chair of their counterpart task force. Teams needed to clearly understand the research and thinking that went into the intent of the recommendations. As teams pressure-tested recommendations to ensure applicability within the parameters of government, they were able to keep the integrity of the intent in mind.

The product of each team was a meticulously vetted document which reviewed the rationale for task force recommendations vis-à-vis the operational realities on the ground. Although details of the task force cost analyses were at times adjusted, the implementation reviews generally supported the business cases with few and minor variances.

The implementation teams worked under four guiding principles, which addressed operations and opportunities. The principles of Governance and Feasibility kept operational reforms within the white lines of legality and practicality. The principles of Cost Savings and Customer Service focused on these objectives as key opportunities of re-engineering.

A number of recurring themes emerged during the individual team deliberations:

- Adopt a center-led model and shared services for enterprise-level functions
- Require systematically generated data which was available, accurate and accessible for management decisions
- Foster a culture of cooperative relationships and coordinated efforts among agencies
- Build solutions that serve for the long-haul

By the time implementation teams were up and running in August 2004, they had about 25 business days to vet the task force recommendations, validate conclusions and draw up options for an action plan. The workload coincided with the run-up to budget hearings, when agency leaders and staffs were scrambling to meet the Governor's new guidelines for performance-based budget requests. Nevertheless, by the Commission's quarterly meeting on October 12, 2004, all four implementation teams stood ready to report.

Their presentations to the Commission made the work ahead seem deceivingly straightforward and simple. Solutions dealing with entangled interfaces and entrenched institutions were reduced to four or five bullets on a PowerPoint slide. The key point was bold and clear to Commission members: Actual plans were underway, on the watch of the Governor's top leadership, to implement CNG recommendations.

THERE WAS ONE INTERESTING DEVIATION between the original Administrative Services implementation report and the presentation made to the Commission. In the first iteration, the team endorsed the CNG task force recommendation to establish a Chief Administrative Officer (CAO) in charge of the shared services model, which included property management, procurement, human resources and technology.

The concept of center-led shared services was unmistakably where Perdue wanted the enterprise system to go, but he didn't want a CAO to take it there. That decision had been made before CNG existed. The COO and CFO were deemed sufficient to manage enterprise services within their reporting agencies and to keep open lines of communication between agency heads and the Governor.

Following extensive dialogue with the Governor just before the CNG meeting, the implementation team collectively revised their report to step back from the CAO and substitute language calling for "strong leadership to drive changes in administrative services." They fully backed the implementation of "a center-led model for shared services" to improve efficiency and customer service, which formed the organizational alignment in place today.

This was the green light for a sweeping reorganization of key functions of bureaucracy to transform the way business is done inside government and ultimately how services are delivered to the public.

GROUND GAME

"Whereas the task force might have preferred to base recommendations solely on how business operates, whether we liked it or not, we recognized that we live and work in a political environment. We knew there would be reasons some things were more feasible or less feasible in government."

LONICE BARRETT, DIRECTOR, GOVERNOR'S OFFICE OF IMPLEMENTATION

The first implementation teams delivered four reports totaling 114 pages. They outlined prescribed actions to go forward and offered caveats about the pitfalls on the path.

Every project lugged some baggage into the implementation process. This was especially true in the early initiatives to realign and centralize administrative services, significant parts of which were in the control of various agencies. The scope of administrative services was so immense that it was split up into individual task forces and implementation teams dealing with procurement, property management and fleet management. Later task forces dealt with human resources. The technology piece went forward independently, as an outsourcing option.

This is where business and government live on different planets. The Commission could make a sound business case for improving any operation in the bureaucracy. But implementing it could not be accomplished with a memo to the company. The state's CEO isn't always empowered to change the order of things "because I say so." Undoing agency assignments and rules authorized by past legislation require amending those statutes. Executive orders which counter previous edicts must pass legal review. Personnel changes that come with reorganization deserve fair handling. Newly created commissioner-level positions with broad authority, such as a State Property Officer, must be ratified by legislation.

Funding was a major matter – always. Nearly all of the Task Force/ Implementation Team recommendations came with a price for modern technologies needed to leap from decades-old tools to 21st Century business systems. Trade-offs between investments and returns could be tricky to nail down.

In the best-case scenarios, projected cost savings would more than repay the upfront expenses of bringing in new technology and highly-trained staff to upgrade a major function of government. Procurement was clearly a case where substantial money was at stake for savings – projections were in range of $100 million a year. Cost/benefit... *Profitable.*

In some areas, the benefit was semi-quantifiable as "cost-avoidance." That's government-speak for Ben Franklin's simple truth that "A penny saved is a penny earned." It is achieved in various ways. One example is shedding assets that are costly to maintain, such as surplus vehicles, to spare further expense. Another is streamlining operations to be more productive without increasing staff and funding. That was the outcome of process improvement in service delivery areas such as driver licensing centers, which cut the customer's average time in-and-out of the bureau from hours to minutes. Cost/benefit... *Sensible.*

And then there was the pure reward of bringing smart practices to create a better-working state government, prouder employees and satisfied customers. Cost/benefit... *Priceless.*

THE IMPLEMENTATION PROCESS WAS NEITHER A STRAIGHT LINE nor a precise line-up of compartmentalized projects that marched in sequence from Point A to Point B. The dedicated-mission model of implementation was a first in government. Typically, commission reports are the end-products, which are handed off to the owner-agency or to a committee of bureaucrats where, it is said, "good ideas go to die."

Barrett invented the implementation process as he went along, led by his instincts for working the system he knew so well. Every project involved a unique set of resources, requirements and personalities. During the Assembly sessions, Barrett's strategy was sheer shoe-leather diplomacy between the Capitol and state offices. He made the daily rounds of committee rooms and legislative offices to persuade, negotiate, hand-hold and be the go-between, smoothing the way for legislation, appropriations and agency participation. Agency heads and even the Governor's policy staff had to be brought along as developments zigged and zagged. Just keeping extraordinarily busy people attentive to the implementation agenda was a fulltime pursuit. Barrett called it assuming the role of "squeaking wheel."

Sweating the small stuff was part of the job description. Any chink in the track could throw off progress indefinitely. Details were hammered out in multiple iterations, so all parties could see the way to a solution.

The director's job was to tend the progress of every project until all the moving parts were in place and working, and the system was adopted into a home agency monitored by the CFO or COO. Afterwards, the implementation office still maintained contact with the principals, troubleshooting issues even years down the road. Barrett, whose propensity is always to drink from the full half of the glass, saw the turning of the culture:

> "There were roadblocks at times – maybe a temporary lack of understanding, the need to change the statute, or a board or commission or agency head we needed to work through to coordinate with clients. But people were willing to listen, if we did our homework and came forward with a reasoned, common-sense approach. We had a tendency to want to go 100 percent, but sometimes we needed to start at 75 percent. We were impatient not to let excuses stop us from going forth."

As a former agency head who had served seven Governors, Barrett had a heart for leaders trying to move with the times.

"Once the concept was okayed and supervision issues were addressed, we counted on agency heads to go forward," Barrett said. "Legislative or budget changes worked through a process, but when we put an agency head in position to act, they were anxious to take leadership and make it happen."

The first rounds of implementation produced substantial fodder for change. Governor Perdue took the stage to announce significant reforms before year-end:

- Frigid gusts slapped the throng of press and guests gathered on the Butler parking deck across from the Capitol on December 15, 2004. A fleet of state-owned Fords created a backdrop for Governor Perdue's announcement of an executive order to count every car in the state and reduce that number 10 percent by June 30, 2005. He also ordered new rules to tighten commuting and restrict personal assignments of government cars.

- The same week, the Governor met reporters at a state warehouse in Atlanta, where surplus property was about to be posted on e-Bay for the first time. On the auction block with office desks, old school band instruments, and a 1954 fire truck was an executive jet that had been grounded in Iowa for nearly a year with a broken wing. Georgia would begin cashing in on the fact that almost anything can be sold on the internet. The fire truck sold for $5,000 to a collector in California, and the plane brought $840,000.

- On December 14, Perdue announced an executive order creating the position of State Property Officer to oversee all buildings, lands and leases in a portfolio approach to real estate management. The SPO would be responsible for developing a public database of all state properties and identifying surplus assets to sell. This would require legislatively merging the management of buildings, lands, leases and construction, which were siloed in four agencies, and putting them under a centralized authority.

Of course, an announcement is only a statement of intention. In politics and poker, you never count your money till the dealing's done. Dealing with the 2005 legislature began the annual challenge of selling reforms which would disrupt the current order, possibly make some administrators mad, and sometimes cost real money.

Barrett understood the virtue in patience:

> "There were countless meetings, conversations and explanations of what was proposed. It was clear that members of the legislature knew changes needed to occur and to make it happen they had to invest in the process. The adage of 'not getting into this situation in a hurry and not getting out of it in a hurry' was so true. And, because of the Governor's strong lobbying and support for the process, the members of the General Assembly also bought in."

THE 2005 LEGISLATIVE SESSION WAS A WATERSHED for modernizing and streamlining government. Floor leaders batted 1.000, bringing home six bills, with none left on base. The Governor held the signing for the first three bills in the Capitol Rotunda, inviting Commission members and agency heads to attend the ceremonies.

→ SENATE BILL 158 codified the Governor's appointment of a State Property Officer and consolidated management of previously overlapping responsibilities for buildings, lands and leasing.

YOU HAVE TO SPEND TO SAVE

One of the toughest sells was the eye-popping appropriations package for procurement transformation. The salesman who clinched the deal was the original initiator of the project, the Commission's task force chair for procurement, Jim Balloun. At the time, he was CEO of Acuity Brands, which had just launched a highly successful procurement modernization project, saving the company over $75 million a year. Balloun said Acuity's procurement managers "were united in their view that they purchase things more effectively than any other company in the industry."

In 2004, when Balloun learned that a Governor's Commission was soliciting private-sector ideas for improving government operations, he called his friend Jim Lientz to talk about Acuity's results with the new technology of internet-enabled auctions. Considering that the state's annual purchasing ran in the $5 billion range, the potential savings of smarter buying technologies and strategies were also eye-popping. CNG formed the task force and asked Balloun to chair. Ultimately, the recommendations called for a clean sweep of the old business methods and installation of a 21st Century procurement operation.

Legislators generally acknowledged the need, but the enormity of the investment in this little-understood niche of government was off-putting and close to being off the table. Balloun volunteered to lobby as a private citizen and met with the Republican leadership caucus.

"I remember sitting at the table with a few senators and representatives reviewing this. I told them it will take $22 million to develop and implement. I also said this figure might seem like a lot of money, but I advised them to either approve the project for the entire $22 million or not at all. If you don't approve the full amount, there's a high chance you'll fail, mess it up, waste the money, and undermine the credibility to do anything. I urged them to take a risk, one that could possibly save them over $100 million a year.

"I was really impressed with the group. They asked good questions. And I was impressed they decided to act."

Commission task forces had estimated that improving space utilization and cost-efficient management would save more than $32 million over four years.

→ HOUSE BILL 312 reformed three major areas of capital asset management. Procurement was centralized to allow the state to leverage volume pricing with more flexibility in negotiations. Fleet management was consolidated and commuting regulations tightened. To increase sales of surplus inventory, agencies were rewarded a cut of the proceeds for turning in unused equipment.

→ HOUSE BILL 275 brought all state retirement plans under the Employee Retirement System to increase the investment growth of employee and state contributions. This was an administrative services-initiated precursor of future Commission task forces in human resources management and pension investments.

→ Later that spring, Perdue signed HOUSE BILL 125 creating the Georgia Tourism Foundation. The non-profit organization enabled the state's public and private resources to be pooled in strategic marketing of Georgia's visitor venues.

→ HOUSE BILL 501 authorized the move of Drivers Services Centers out of the Department of Motor Vehicles in order to make the license process faster, friendlier and easier. Citizens cheered.

→ While the legislature was in session, the Commission's Accounts Receivables Task Force reported recommendations to improve cash management and collections of delinquent accounts. As recommended by the task force, HOUSE BILL 293 created the position of Georgia's first State Accounting Officer to realign the financial reporting and system responsibilities under a centralized chief of accounting. In 2006, Georgia met the deadline for the annual federal audit report for the first time since 1991.

→ The legislature also approved the funding packages for procurement transformation and a fleet management system.

EXECUTION

"It starts with people, but then you need to have a government structure that is well understood and communicated. It must ensure freedom of creativity and the liberty to fail. If you don't have the freedom to fail, you're not going to 'get stretched,' and you will stay at safe. That's the recipe for lack of progress."
GOVERNOR SONNY PERDUE

The enabling legislation was a milestone on the road to implementation and the destination of results. The initiatives could go nowhere without the statutory green light, but there was still a long and winding road ahead and a journey taken step-by-step. Each project had to work through reorganization of responsibilities, leadership changes and administratively building systems with new tools. Timelines, cost projections and evaluation criteria for outcomes were developed. Metrics were a primary component: What was the objective to be measured? How could processes be changed to get those results?

On the ground were agency leaders and their key staff, working out the details of transitions from multiple-agency control of assets to enterprise systems. For the right administrator with an aptitude for process re-engineering, the challenge was a stimulating venture in problem-solving and seeking best practices from innovators. But they needed to know that their leaders had their backs.

They had that in the business-minded chief executive. Perdue wanted to create a culture that valued enterprising administrators and employees up and down the ranks.

"Leadership is about making people believe they can do more than they ever thought they could, believing in them, giving them responsibilities, trusting them with those responsibilities, being hands off. My management style is one of trust, inspiration, motivation, believing in people and encouraging from that perspective.

"One of the things I believe I am gifted with is observing people and building on their strengths. Find the good people in the field in which you want them to operate and let them go. You've got to give people an ownership of the final product, and that's something we haven't done a very good job of in the past. Whether they clean the floor or water the flowers, it's important they carry a sense of ownership in the overall delivery."

Perdue personally enjoyed the free-flowing exchange of ideas, posing pointed questions and achieving consensus. "From a leadership standpoint, what gives me fulfillment is getting people together and collectively accomplishing things from a team perspective much more than any one could have accomplished individually. A good leader has to cultivate an atmosphere where all can speak their minds and at the end of the day still have the team spirit when a decision is made."

Barrett said the monthly meetings of the CFO and COO reports inculcated agency heads with two assurances: first, they all had a stake in the success of the enterprise, and second, they had the support of the executive team to do what was necessary to change. The effect of that cannot be underestimated, in Barrett's opinion as a former agency head and implementation chief.

"That was the first time in my entire career that there were regularly scheduled staff meetings where issues were discussed, suggestions were made, input was received, and direct messages were heard in the presence of my peers," he said. "Best-managed state was drilled home. It was a lofty goal. We discussed how to do it and how to know when it's done. It set the stage for implementing change throughout the series of 24 Commission task force initiatives."

Agency heads were expected to follow suit in communicating with their team. Barrett believed it may have been the first time in Georgia's modern governing history where this sort of dialogue was standard operating procedure between agency heads and their direct reports as a group.

"It was my experience in state government that the corporate structure of top-down direction is efficient from the leadership through the second level," Barrett said. "Where enthusiasm typically died was in that third or fourth level. But when an agency head is able to go back to the departments and talk about ideas and plans, it pushes information down through the ranks and gives people a first-person opportunity to hear and participate."

Lientz said the executive team was acutely conscious that consistency of message was critical.

"This was not the crisis du jour. Somebody has to be constantly on it," the COO said. "The Governor has to be consistent, the chiefs have to be consistent and not allow the politics of the hour to take over. That means political forces inside or outside the Administration."

Carl Swearingen worked with agency heads as CNG liaison to the 2005 Customer Service Task Force.

"In most cases, the processes have been embedded for years. And you have to go in and not just chisel away. You have to blow them up.

"The challenge became, "What could the agency heads do within each structure with such a demand for other things?" With that came the empowerment of people within the agency, and that's one of the true benefits. It connects back to the culture. Someone asks for my ideas and input, and, wow, they let me go try it! Even if we fail – meaning that door won't open the way we thought it would – the credit then goes to the agency leadership for continuing to pound at the issue. They wanted to come back to the Governor and say, 'Solution A didn't work, but we developed Solution X, and it's better than A.' Once you get to that level of excitement, you've turned the corner."

When the new Department of Driver Services began opening doors to a fast-moving, no-hassle licensing process, the Governor remembers experiencing, for the first time, the "joy" of customer service.

"Under the auspices of a wonderful young leader, Greg Dozier, this department – newly created, but staffed by existing employees – began providing extraordinarily better customer service. As a result, the employees were happier because the customers were happier.

"And it was not a false happiness. It was true joy over what had been and could be accomplished. Watching that principle of human nature gave me great fulfillment."

WHOSE BALL?

"I pride myself on being a facts-based decision maker, and I find we run into a lot of politics."

GOVERNOR SONNY PERDUE

The first round of successes – markers on the way to next steps – became the template for the task force initiatives that followed over the next five years. They also harbored intimations of the tensions that would come between executive and legislative priorities.

"In our dealings with the legislature in the first year, there was a lot of willingness to support the effort because there was a recognition that things needed to improve, even if they didn't know details of how far behind we were," Barrett said. "There was a willingness to fund and provide legislative tools and a desire to support the Governor in an initiative that was the right thing to do.

"That said, when changes actually began, the fallout of doing business differently put a few legislators in the position of choosing between individual interests and the larger interest of improving government."

Legislators had a big bone to pick with the principle of "spending money to save money." In the case of procurement, modernization required a drastic overhaul, led by a consulting firm which had designed and implemented successful systems in other states. Georgia was paying billions of dollars for thousands of goods and services purchased by hundreds of agencies and had no ability to analyze spending, the cost and value of the purchases, or the proficiency of the operation. The firm would be contracted for a three-year procurement transformation to produce a turnkey system projected to generate an estimated $135 million in savings in the first year of full operation. Still, the upfront cost was almost $20 million for the contract, for hiring professionally trained staff and for buying new technology for online procurement processes.

Additional funding was required to tie the fleet management system into the state's PeopleSoft accounting system and to build a database for property management.

Legislators wanted to know when they would start counting payback dollars for the appropriation. Barrett said lobbying for appropriations always raised that question and "forced us into a corner of saying how much we would save."

"Looking back, one of the things we didn't do right was putting too much emphasis on the money saved and not the efficiency, customer service, assembly of information and streamlining. It took money to modernize, to staff and to make institutional changes that were necessary to do business in the 21st Century.

"Everything we talked about came down to the payback value. We could count dollars for car and land sales, but not for costs like maintenance. The single biggest anxiety was how to demonstrate efficiencies and the importance of the improvements.

"CNG was never sufficiently acknowledged for the value that didn't have savings attached to it."

THE IMPLEMENTATION OFFICE MADE A SERIOUS ATTEMPT to quantify and verify savings, through an Internal Financial Validation Committee formed in 2006. The committee brought accounting expertise from inside and outside government to assess from agency records the dollars saved by cutting costs, or spared by avoidance, or redirected to higher priorities, or recovered in revenues. The committee was chaired by J. Don Edwards, J.M. Tull Professor of Accounting at the University of Georgia, and nationally renowned in his field. Their primary mission was to establish savings methodologies, estimates and documentation for functional areas. They also monitored spending patterns and identified potential and actual savings.

For FY 2006, the validation committee affirmed that Commission initiatives had generated $21.9 million in cost savings available for the FY07/FY08 budget cycle. The savings were squeezed primarily from bundled contract pricing on a variety of maintenance supplies, renegotiating high-priced leases to market value and reduction of telecommunications rates. The total did not include prior-year savings, cost avoidance or local government discounts on contract pricing. It also didn't count the nearly $18 million in proceeds from the sale of surplus real estate in the previous year. Also in the wings was nearly $2.7 million in general obligation bond funds the State Property Officer identified in construction projects that were cancelled or never built. Those would be available for reallocation.

By December 2006, validated savings had returned $10 million in sales revenues to the state treasury and made $16.7 million available to the legislature for the amended FY07 and FY08 budgets. Perdue intended to let agencies keep a portion of their savings to redirect the funds to program priorities. The idea was to raise their incentive to participate aggressively in the cost-saving programs.

Instead, when the legislature got a look at the figures for redirection, agencies' budgets were cut accordingly, and all of the funds were swept for House and Senate projects. Agencies which had worked hardest to save paid the highest price.

"I wanted to be transparent, and showed the legislature a report card of CNG savings, and told them we had promised managers a portion of that. But they scooped it out to use for their own purposes," said a disgusted Governor.

It was the first and last CNG validation report delivered to the legislature, and the committee was quietly disbanded. The Implementation Office continued to track and tally results of task force-initiated projects and report to the Commission, which offered a more discerning audience for the information. The business executives understood the value of leveraging purchase power in contracts, running cost-effective operations, and instituting efficiencies that translated to better customer satisfaction.

The legislature ran hot and cold on Commission initiatives, at times based on who was or was not getting along with the Governor. Who "owns" savings continued to be a bone of contention. The Implementation Office's avoidance of reporting itemized savings – because they would be subtracted from agency budgets – fed the perception that the Commission's efforts were a bust, not delivering on promised revenues. But inside agencies, the savings were accruing and being used to offset requests for funding increases.

The notion of sweeping lump sums of savings was based on a major fallacy about how funds accrued. Seven- and eight-figure savings projections may be spread over a multi-year contract, among many departments buying the item, and the quantity of items purchased in one year compared to another. The savings are real, and eventually the averages are likely to meet the projection. But scooping the individual savings from each department takes going door-to-door with a tin cup, not digging into a pile of cash with a steam shovel.

CHANGE SET OFF A NUMBER OF SKIRMISHES over money and control. When the procurement process began to move to strategic sourcing – based on volume buying, typically from large vendors – there was a hue and cry from hometown businesses which counted on profits from sales to local colleges and state offices. District legislators questioned a process they saw as unfairly penalizing local businesses which couldn't compete on price and volume. They were willing to compromise state savings to accommodate constituents. On another front, the 2006 CNG Aviation Task Force had proposed consolidating the state's "four little air forces" of helicopters and planes acquired over the years by individual agencies. The proposed aviation authority would provide safer, streamlined services for all air missions with fewer, newer aircraft under professionally managed training and maintenance programs. Agencies enlisted friends in the chambers to fight giving up their air command. Their opposition grounded aviation legislation for three years, until the final day of the 2009 session.

The control of administrative and management functions straddles the legislative and executive branches. Ultimately, it is the Governor who is the boss of the agency heads, overseeing government operations year-round, while legislators are back home dealing with their own businesses. Perdue was determined to manage the transformation initiatives at the executive level because, he said, "We need change to be a process, not an event."

The Governor continued to drive the point that sustained effort was making a difference in the state's fiscal future. In his 2008 budget message to the joint session, he noted that the "mere two percent increase (in the amended FY08 budget) represents the smallest increase in state funds that I have recommended to the legislature since Georgia recovered from the recession in the beginning of my first term.

"This relatively small increase can be attributed to efficiencies and cost avoidance techniques implemented through the Commission for a New Georgia and efforts carried out by state agencies. Soon Georgia will be recognized as the best-managed state in the nation."

In 2008, the Senate decided to create its own "value-in-government" committee, which after two years presented a report on ways the state could manage its business more efficiently. Most were reiterations of Commission recommendations already underway.

NO TIMEOUTS

"When the old system is turned off, everybody applauds the result. They now possessed the team, skills and tools to cope with the dramatic changes in their marketplace."

JEFF STRANE, DIRECTOR OF IMPLEMENTATION, 2007-10

Major implementation initiatives had gathered steam from 2005 legislation and appropriations. Meanwhile back at CNG, task forces had been pumping out more reports and recommendations – a total of 10 in 2004. Six were addressed by legislation in the 2005 session. The four that were ramping up next included Leadership Development, Strategic Industries, Competitiveness, and Workforce Development.

In 2005, five more task forces followed not far behind: Receivables, Public

GETTING IT DONE...

Lonice Barrett (*left*) and Jeff Strane (*right*) carried the implementation of 130 Commission recommendations to a 98 percent completion rate since the Governor's Office of Implementation was established in 2004.

Finance Options, Customer Service, State Health Benefits, and delivery of quality care for mentally and physically disabled Georgians at their community service bureaus.

When the Implementation Office completed its first full year in Fall 2005, there were 15 task force initiatives underway. Each project had its own cross-agency administrative planning team which was organized, supported and urged on by Barrett and his Deputy Director Sid Johnson, who was experienced in state administration and business executive development. The workload might be imagined as a pair of one-armed paperhangers covering 15 rooms at the same time – with flypaper. Letting go of projects took months and even years, while new task force recommendations were coming on board every quarter.

Barrett retired in 2006. He was succeeded by Johnson who left in 2007 for a position in the Carl Vinson Institute of Government. When Jeff Strane took over as implementation director in 2007, the number had grown to 19 active projects, adding risk management, aviation consolidation, service delivery regions, and transportation costs. Strane knew the ways of bureaucracy. He had more than 20 years experience in state and local governments, including seven years with the Georgia Department of Economic Development where he was the director of the Science and Technology Office. He went about his work with laid-back persistence.

"When task force recommendations went into the implementation process, the work had just begun," Strane said. "We always started at ground zero, knowing that a combination of technology, leadership, culture and process changes were going to be needed."

"Many times we had to convince agency leadership and staff to go with us – almost blindly – through a well-established process to break down institutional barriers and look with fresh eyes at what they actually did and to consider and ultimately integrate new processes òr systems. This usually meant working on both old and new systems until we were ready to move to the new platform.

"Our job was to remain with the project – sometimes pushing, other times empathizing with how hard change is, but always keeping the drumbeat going that the end game is worth it. In the short run, it doubles the work to keep business going while you are trying to move to the new process or system. But when the old system is turned off, everybody applauds the result. They saw significant improvement in their ability to provide better service, make better decisions and better manage with accurate data. The employees had become a better-trained, more committed staff with a set of new skills."

That outcome could take several years through phases of funding, technology integration, new leadership, staff training, and troubleshooting. Strane cites the fleet management initiative which started in 2004; the system was finally in operation with a professionally qualified director in 2007.

MULTI-TASKING A SCORE OF PROJECTS was made manageable by fresh, professional leadership in the agencies and the introduction or extension of IT systems to network enterprise functions. One of the notable developments driving the Administration's effectiveness was an influx of top management professionals educated and experienced in the areas they would administer. Those from the private sector were already on the same page as the business-led task forces. Jim Lientz said the state had become a magnet for management-level professionals "who saw this as something rewarding they wanted to be part of."

"There were private-sector folks who caught the vision," Lientz said, adding that "The paradox was they thought it was going to be easy because they knew how to deal with this in the business environment."

As implementation carried into the Governor's second term after the 2006 election, the task forces began to morph from tactical operations to a broader scan of issues which had a business side relevant to strategic decisions. Transportation and Freight and Logistics task forces contributed business analyses instrumental to the larger statewide transportation planning process. State-sponsored research was producing intellectual property which needed a higher profile in the commercial market. There was special potential in bio-science where Georgia ranked eighth as a center for entrepreneurial companies. Geographically, the state's service delivery regions didn't compare in size, funding and quality of services, leaving many counties as outliers in statewide planning.

THE IMPLEMENTATION OFFICE ALWAYS SAW ITSELF AS "THE CLOSER." It closed the loop on responsibility for progress in instituting innovation. It closed the project with a successful handoff to a home agency. And it was the closer in the end-game of embedding Commission recommendations for business innovation, a culture of customer service, and strategic economic planning into the fabric of state government.

―――

"What's unique to me about this whole undertaking was we actually implemented the recommendations, and they have been tracked. That, coupled with the Governor's desire to be one of the best-managed states in the country, gave everyone a common goal to work towards. The breakdown of the silos helped. It was like lining up the dominos. The opportunity to work together as a team, to get rid of some of those barriers has been the winning formula for changing state government. Changing state government is not just an administrative change. It's really a change in culture."

CELESTE OSBORNE, DEPUTY CHIEF FINANCE OFFICER (2003 - 2009)

CHAPTER FOUR TAKE AWAY...

Implementation is only as strong as the will of the CEO, who makes it understood as a no-excuses priority.

. . . .

The infrastructure for implementation is built into the organizational relationship between the executive team and agency leaders, as individuals and as a group.

. . . .

Accountability for implementing innovation is owned by the executive team and a part of the performance contract of their direct reports. That becomes the model for agency heads within their divisions.

. . . .

Continual and consistent communication of goals and plans keeps players on task and contributing to possibility-thinking.

. . . .

Risk and trust are two sides of the same coin. Administrators stepping out as problem-solvers need to know their leaders have their backs.

. . . .

Implementation pivots on the right champion – placed at the highest level of government – whose sole job is turning recommendations to projects and staying on point until they are stand-alone operations.

. . . .

Implementation is a team sport. Never underestimate the power of an aspirational goal to rally expectations, focus energies and create success.

. . . .

Implementers will always face the challenge of entrenched interests, but at the end of the day, unwavering, willful efforts for the right reasons will overcome obstacles and outlast obstructors.

. . . .

The inclusive and institutional nature of implementation presents the opportunity to influence both the business and culture of government as no other single factor.

CHAPTER FIVE

INSTITUTIONALIZING THE BEST-MANAGED STATE: BUREAUCRACY WITH A BUSINESS BRAIN

Governor Sonny Perdue spent seven years re-engineering the workings of state government. It took dismantling a decades-old contraption of parts appended to agencies and redeveloping a 21st Century public enterprise managed with business sense in a culture of public service.

The synergy of innovation and implementation drove change with phenomenal momentum and reach. Folks who've served the state for decades say they never experienced reform which moved so fast and far through government.

In the most recent national management ratings, Georgia made the greatest strides in the country, jumping nearly 20 places to the top five states.

Sustaining a business-minded enterprise in a culture of service is now Georgia's to use or lose.

...LIKE A FLYWHEEL

BUILT TO LAST

THE SCORECARD

"Sustaining progress is like a flywheel. We're exerting enough external energy on the wheel of state government so it's turning with such force that it takes more energy to stop it than to continue it."

GOVERNOR SONNY PERDUE

Roll the credits on achievements initiated by the Commission for A New Georgia, and there is no question that the State of Georgia today is a far more effective, efficient, accountable and customer-friendly government than it was in 2003.

The question is whether that state will go forward as the new norm for managing government or revert to the old business-as-usual.

Through two Perdue terms, the business and culture of bureaucracy have been steadily pulled into the force field of the transformation flywheel, powered by new laws, aggressive leadership, cutting edge technologies, best practices and a high priority on service.

The Governor didn't predict the 2008 crash, but he knew to prepare for the coming reality of sustainable government. He is proud of his team's response. "We have leaders with a can-do spirit suggesting ideas and doing things that would impress any business operation," Perdue said. "That connects to the value of our decision to prepare for a more efficient operation able to survive tough times."

If the Great Recession burned a lesson into the annals of governing, it is this: Governments must stay on top of the total cost of their obligations, current and future, in order to balance projected expenditures against the spectrum of revenue scenarios.

Georgia is acutely aware that its triple-A credit rating is always at stake. Convincing New York rating agencies that sound management prevails in dire times is critical to Georgia's continued access to capital at the lowest cost of borrowing. The value translation for citizens is in funding for highways, schools and public works – which also circulates dollars for economic growth and jobs.

THE DEVIL IS IN THE DETAILS, and the details are in the data. The Perdue Administration made it their mission to build the state's capacity for data-mining and information-management. That became the basis for understanding the actual and anticipated cost of government and asserting measures to manage it. Perdue embraced the realities of data to inform best-value decisions about investing tax dollars and divesting costly surplus assets. Those capabilities will be passed on to the next administration.

To undergird the state's financial infrastructure, Perdue prevailed upon the legislature to double the percentage of each previous year's budget which could be invested in the state reserve as a hedge against downturns – which followed with shocking speed and severity. He asserted policies to constrain the ballooning obligations for employee benefits which would overwhelm the state's financial capacity and pass intolerable debt to future generations.

The Commission for A New Georgia's business-based recommendations posed a sharp contrast to practices in place when the Governor took office. Strategies to implement CNG measures were designed to exert force on the flywheel, driving new ways of doing business inexorably into the operations and culture of the enterprise.

The flywheel effect is a powerful force in the short run, but over time it's vulnerable to the drag of deferred management. The national watchdog of government performance is watching Georgia as a bellwether of serious, sustained management transformation.

A DOZEN WAYS GEORGIA'S GOVERNMENT IS WORKING BETTER

Fragmented functions are now a cohesive unit, and responsibilities are centered in a lead agency for each management area.

Sophisticated business systems and professionally qualified administrators are streamlining processes and bringing usable data to decision-making.

Agency leaders have emerged from silos to work as a team on common issues of state business.

Georgia can account for all of its major assets, tracking costs of ownership as the basis for informed management.

A new spending analytics tool – a national model invented by Georgia's purchasing division – reveals what departments buy and pay to procure billions of dollars worth of supplies, equipment and services.

Nearly a half-billion dollars in delinquent taxes, fees and reimbursements have been collected using new strategies to flush out evaders.

Millions of dollars are saved every year on state insurance claims through a comprehensive program for loss and accident prevention.

Program-based budgeting and performance-based pay are tying resources to state priorities and measurable outcomes.

A performance-based HR system has positioned the State of Georgia as an employer of choice in the competitive market for high-caliber job seekers.

State employees are part of the team, rethinking processes to better serve citizens and make their jobs more productive.

Waiting lines, calls-on-hold and turnaround time for transactions have been cut dramatically.

Georgians can now call one number and get live assistance to reach any state service.

BUILT TO LAST

"Georgia has placed a high priority and focus on effective management. The challenge for Georgia will be to continue to institutionalize and build upon the management changes that are beginning to take hold."

PEW CENTER ON THE STATES, 2008 "CHARTING THE COURSE FOR EXCELLENCE"

The Pew Center is the nationally recognized arbiter of best-managed governments. Its executive summary of Georgia's evaluation in the 2008 Government Performance Project ratified the state's claim to change:

"Georgia has made significant performance improvements over the past few years, thanks to Governor Sonny Perdue's focus on management and customer service. His Commission for A New Georgia, comprising task forces composed of 300 private-sector representatives, has effected change and created efficiencies in a wide range of management areas.

"...Governor Perdue and his administration have strengthened the state's performance culture. A focus on results has spread through state agencies, and many employees understand how their performance relates to agency and state strategic objectives. The state has strong fiscal-management practices."

The significant performance improvements referenced by Pew each required a special combination of forces converging from the executive, legislative, administrative and employee sectors and in some cases from external partners. Technology was pivotal. The point has been to use every means at hand to implant transformative measures so securely into operations that progress cannot roll backwards.

EXECUTIVE LEADERSHIP can be the strongest or the weakest factor in managing for performance. A chief executive who possesses strong managerial instincts is the visionary and champion of a new order and aligns the organization, resources and directives to see it through. Sonny Perdue deliberately chose his battles and leaders and never abandoned his post as general of the campaign for a best-managed state.

When Commission members, task force chairs and administration chiefs were asked to choose the most important factor in achieving success, every answer started with the leadership of Sonny Perdue. After that, the citations held equal import:

- The Administration's appointment of the Chief Operating Officer and Chief Financial Officer to organize the agenda for new business and mobilize agency leaders to implement innovation;
- the creation of the Commission for A New Georgia to bring business acumen and professional integrity to the reform effort;
- and the implementation initiatives which instituted change and recharged the enthusiasm of the Commission to continue its work.

Concern was expressed over the prospect that a different breed of chief executive may show up and relegate management matters to a lower tier of governing. The flywheel at some point winds down and gathers rust.

The unpredictability of future governors' management interest and knowledge makes implementation measures a matter of serious strategy. Dredging old business methods out of silos and ensconcing smart management in law, learning and practice is intended to establish an environment where continuous improvement becomes the new business-as-usual. Perdue worked steadfastly to leave that environment as his legacy.

The governor's role is large-and-in-charge. It is the CEO's prerogative to announce the vision, ensconce it on the priority agenda, organize the administration to ensure action, engage powerful allies, lay institutional groundwork through legislation and executive orders, communicate goals to the enterprise, back up change agents, celebrate success and keep all eyes on the prize. Perdue did all of those.

.Transforming a big government is always tough and tedious and often thankless. The reality is that the governor is the only person in the state with the visibility, authority and a four-year contract to do the job.

THE LEGISLATURE is the enabler and enactor of institutional change. From 2005 to 2010, a series of bills set in motion the transition of key functions and assets to center-led management. Legislation was required to move fragmented responsibilities from multiple agencies and consolidate authority in an overarching agency. This was key to the historic reform of property management after repeated recommendations by past commissions.

Legislators likewise enabled enterprise-level operation of the vehicle fleet, aviation services and procurement. By statute, the State Personnel Administration took over statewide governance of HR policy and systems.

Prior to 2005 Georgia was the only state without a central accounting function. Legislation was passed to create the first State Accounting Office, instituting coherence in financial systems and reporting.

These actions laid the foundation for enterprise management as the business model for governing.

Best practices were enabled by amending legal restrictions in diverse operational areas. An example was a new law authorizing purchasing agents to negotiate lower pricing through bidding rounds rather than simply accepting quotes at face value.

Legislators responded to customer-focused initiatives, appropriating start-up funds for a 1-800 call center. They supported the Governor's plan to break up the department of motor vehicles and create a separate division for drivers-licensing to relieve public frustration with hours-long waits. It was the biggest customer service coup of the decade.

The legislature also extended the management reforms to service-delivery at the regional and local levels. Legislation supplanted unevenly apportioned and funded regional development centers with a new organization of regional commissions. Districts were equalized with redrawn boundaries, an equitable funding formula and stronger local oversight. The act imposed accountability audits of comprehensive planning and the level of services in districts. The new districts will play a major role in developing regional consensus for transportation planning.

The final piece of legislation in 2010 established in law the Governor's Office of Workforce Development, created by executive order in 2005. The office has built a strong record of helping communities certify a work-ready employment base, which is a draw for companies prospecting new locations.

In all, 18 pieces of legislation advanced by the Perdue Administration have embedded major Commission recommendations in government. Undoing legislated acts is doable, but not done capriciously.

LEADERSHIP AND MANAGEMENT responsibility for implementing reform was on the agenda of every direct report to the chiefs of operations and finance.

It wasn't only processes that were changing. So were the people involved, either by turnover or by training. New agency heads, many from outside government, took over the Department of Administrative Services, the State Purchasing Office, the State Property Office, the Georgia Technology Authority, the State Personnel Administration, the State Accounting Office and the divisions of Risk Management and Fleet Management.

The administration moved toward professionalizing agency leadership. Applicable industry-specific experience was preferred over state service credits. Executives and practitioners were recruited from corporate operations to infuse their expertise and bypass the learning curve.

Not all fresh-faced leaders came from outside. An up-and-coming generation of talented administrators who were serving in state government – tested and trusted by the Governor's executive team – was tapped to undertake the challenges of some high-wire transformation projects. Their common denominator was fearing only fear itself.

Yale-educated Patrick Moore, at age 33, was appointed executive director of the Georgia Technology Authority. He put together the consolidation and outsourcing of the state's IT operations and telecomm network to industry giants IBM and AT&T. The contracts totaled over $1.2 billion, and the conversion would put the state on a par with business enterprises which continuously upgrade their technology capabilities. Meanwhile, the Driver Services reorganization to a stand-alone agency was turned over to Greg Dozier, 34, a budget analyst with a degree in criminal justice. His challenge was to take the slow and aggravating process experienced by seven million Georgians a year and make it faster, friendlier and easier.

Top leadership change also brought higher standards of qualification into the management tier and through the ranks. At all staff levels, training in new business systems was a critical component of every transformation. People who wanted to stay with the program had to get certified in their area. The spinoff benefit was a proliferation of new ways to deliver training to employees all over the state through internet learning modules and online classes. In the procurement transformation, web-based seminars were extended to suppliers as well as purchasing agents to expedite the transition to a fully-informed working relationship. The Office of Customer Service offered a strong training component for front-line employees, and more than 10,000 signed up for classes on line. Learning was contagious, and employees wanted to catch it.

Leadership development and succession was identified early on by the Commission as a gap the state must bridge to cross over to a performance culture. GE Vice President and CNG charter member John Rice explained the emphasis:

> "The Governor and the Commission understood that you can have the biggest, best, boldest ideas, but if don't have a process for developing talent, training, and succession planning, you are going to be left with a mediocre team – and almost by definition, mediocre results. There's no organization that doesn't need to think about the caliber of its leadership development processes."

The first-in-the-state Georgia Leadership Institute was inaugurated in 2005 to initiate a pipeline of prospects to fill the management void left by retiring Boomers. The institute later expanded training tiers from supervisor-level to commissioners.

In concert with the State Personnel performance system, upward mobility for ambitious employees comes in both pay and promotion. Tangible rewards encourage the most promising public servants to keep contributing their best work to state government – and keep their shoulders to the flywheel. The newly structured HR benefits package plays to the rising generation of employees and future leaders who prefer better pay on the near horizon than better retirement 30 years down the road.

Team Georgia fields about 100,000 employees covering bases all over the state. The Pew Center calls them the "living core of government." Pew's 2008 evaluation singled out Georgia's People Performance for the state's only "A" (A-minus) in the four categories of management.

Employees may be perceived as downstream on the food chain, but the relatively small corps of leaders is dependent on those 100,000 team members returning the investment in their value.

Culture change is the hearts-and-minds piece of institutionalizing a best-managed state. The personnel administration has focused on the worth of the employee as an indispensible individual on Team Georgia. CNG's 2004 Administrative Task Force suggested employees needed their own website as a portal to information, services and internal communication. The TeamGeorgia intranet was launched in 2005 and has become the primary self-service access point for employees to view their records and manage their benefits. The online *Georgia Statement* is published monthly to keep employees on the same page about news in state government, advice for professional development and features on high-performing workers.

The Customer Service movement has been equal parts invention and inspiration for employees. The genius of the approach is in inviting the people who do the jobs to join problem-solvers and project managers in upgrading service and performance. Rapid Process Improvement teams work with agency champions and line employees to trace the snafus and straighten the way for more efficiency and less frustration, on both the serving and receiving ends of transactions. The learning experience for employees increases their value as team members in a culture of accountability.

Capping the revitalization of the state workforce, celebration of exceptional service became a regular event. The Governor presented awards at an annual ceremony, and year-round a series of emails and display cards spotlighted employees who use their individual jobs to deliver better service. Employee-satisfaction surveys stayed on the upside, despite furloughs and pay freezes.

Embedding people power in transformation is the secret weapon of change.

TECHNOLOGY'S ROLE cannot be overstated in re-engineering business systems from paper-pushing procedures to strategic management. Actual loss is incurred when a $20 billion enterprise is lagging or lacking in the tools to run multi-million dollar business operations.

In 2003, state government was not without thousands of desktop computers that stored all kinds of records and information – most going nowhere beyond their department. Technology developments have systematically advanced connectivity and information management so 100-plus data centers can feed into central repositories that interface with programs in agencies. In financial management, PeopleSoft became the common accounting platform for revenues, receivables, cash management and a budget network for executive and legislative branches. Programs have also automated administrative processes allowing departments to redirect or reduce staff. Telecommunications and searchable databases serve customers who call the 1-800 information line, which is answered by operators tapping into an online encyclopedia of

WHY CNG WORKED: STRATEGIES FOR SUCCESS

LEADERSHIP

GOVERNOR'S VISION AND INVOLVEMENT: Innovation begins at the top.

PRIVATE SECTOR PARTNERS: Respected executives who lead high-performing organizations focus fresh perspective and enterprise thinking on the workings of government.

STRONG LEGISLATIVE SUPPORT: Forward-thinking legislators who understand 21st Century change invest the necessary resources in transformation technologies and initiatives.

ORGANIZATION AND FUNDING

PRIVATELY FUNDED, NON-PROFIT: The Commission operates with the independence needed to manage the politics of change.

PRO BONO CONSULTING SUPPORT: Donated technical services and project management keep initiatives on track, enabling task forces to make best use of members' expertise and experience.

OPERATIONS

BROAD: Task Force members bring expertise and experience from a diversity of business operations throughout the state – expertise at no expense.

CITIZEN INVOLVEMENT: 24 Task Forces involved more than 400 citizens in direct service to their state government.

NIMBLE: Multiple task forces work on different issues to keep change churning. New task forces can be dispatched as issues arise.

RAPID: Task Forces produce recommendations in about 90 days to expedite action.

RESULTS-FOCUSED: Recommendations are designed to be actionable and measurable.

GOVERNMENT-WIDE: Innovation and improvement are strategic and systematic.

LEAN: The Commission is staffed by one executive-on-loan and one CNG-paid assistant.

IMPLEMENTATION

ACCESS AND ACCOUNTABILITY: The Implementation Director reports to the Governor, ensuring high-visibility initiatives, agency cooperation and responsibility for progress.

TEAMWORK: Cross-agency work groups focus on implementing improvement enterprise-wide, doing the right work in the right way and measuring success.

REAL RESULTS: Demonstrated successes and documented savings continually inspire innovation.

hundreds of services. Enterprise-level recovery systems now back up all state data in secure servers in case of catastrophic breakdown in any segment of government.

The point is that state-of-the-art technology has been bought and embedded in government operations which can now capture and share information vital to management of the enterprise. The state's critical systems are secured to ensure business continuity in almost any scenario.

In terms of the flywheel, installed technologies are the main engine. Once running, they cannot be thrown into reverse without ridiculous consequences. That is why it was imperative to choose and invest in the right technology, built to be built upon.

CONTRACTED PARTNERS tend to be overlooked as agents of transformation. They bring the full weight of expertise and experience to systems that meet the state's needs and stand up to continuously changing and improving business methods. A prime example is procurement partner A.T. Kearney, which designed a system that brought together the latest technologies, proven strategies, staffing and training protocols and best practices in the known world of purchasing management. A venture of this magnitude could never have flown as a do-it-yourself agency project of one-off systems pushing along incremental changes.

Big league partners wield the tools it takes for a holistic overhaul of business-as-usual.

SCORECARD

"If you're not keeping score, you're just practicing."
COACH VINCE LOMBARDI

The Commission's 24 task forces generated 130 recommendations. The first task force reported in April 2004, the last in January 2009. Some called for sweeping change and a total transformation of how the state did business in a major management area. Others wrote specific prescriptions for best practices to improve an existing system. Many recommendations required legislative action that put the implementation timetable on the general assembly cycle – and in the case of the Aviation Authority held up action for three years. Extensive transformations could take extended periods to implement full operation. Beyond implementation, always working on updating and improving systems is a natural part of the new norm of continuous improvement. The ever-present question is, "How can we do this better, cheaper, easier?"

That said, 127 recommendations on the scorecard have been checked off – meaning substantive action has been taken to implement the recommendation, and results have come forth or are on track.

Governor Perdue delivered on 98 percent of his promise to the Commission.

What happened to the three proposals left on the table? The economy happened to two finance recommendations which would have liberalized pension investments in higher-risk funds and encouraged investment of state funds in venture capital as a public finance option. Historically a conservative investor, Georgia was fresh from the recession of 2003 when the Public Finance Task Force recommendation was advanced, and the state was facing down the recession of 2008 when the Investment Strategies Task Force reported. Business people understand market-driven decisions.

The recommendation by the Aviation Task Force to replace all federal surplus aircraft turned out to be financially unfeasible during the budget killings in 2009 and 2010. In a better future, those aging assets will be replaced.

The checked recommendations don't show the initiatives which grew out of implementation work. One is the consolidation of all travel. This is a moneymaker for the state, which spends $100 million on transportation and lodging for state travel. The new system will leverage the agencies' consolidated buying power for airline tickets and accommodations.

Other programs are still to yield their potential return. Georgia's brand new database of bio-research patents and scientists is being expanded to include other sciences. The freight-and-logistics innovation center is coalescing the strengths and potential of Georgia's shipping industries, including the nation's fastest growing seaport, the world's busiest airport, and one of North America's top rail distribution centers.

IN THE QUEST TO BE A BEST-MANAGED STATE, Georgia has been fortunate to draw on the best thinking of executives, practitioners and consultants who know how to manage for success. Their advice was free to Georgia. The only string attached was to use the advice to make government a better value for its citizens.

Governor Sonny Perdue shares his legacy of "leaving the state better" with the Commission for A New Georgia and hundreds of Georgians who believed with him that Georgia could be the best-managed state in the nation and did the work to make it happen – and to endure.

"The Commission for A New Georgia exerted the energy, expertise and enthusiasm to create momentum for change. Our plan was not a blitz, but a building process. Our intention has been to rediscover the best qualities of government and to embed those in an enduring culture of sound business management, accountability for stewardship of public resources and a spirit of service. That is how government creates value for its citizens.

We will never exhaust the need for continuous improvement, measuring results and holding ourselves accountable. My expectation is that every administration which follows will see value in managing Georgia's government by those principles."

SONNY PERDUE, GOVERNOR OF GEORGIA

CHAPTER SIX

RESULTS: TRANSFORMING BUREAUCRACY TO BUSINESS MODEL

In its own way, this chapter faces the challenge which confronted the task forces and implementers: So much stuff to deal with, so little time and space. A full accounting of all 24 task forces – whose stories are individual and contributions are unique – is simply too much for one volume. "Gone With the Wind: A New Day for Government" is out of the question.

Therefore, the strategy is divide-and-condense. Task force topics are clustered in three categories: 1) managing assets, finances and cost-drivers, 2) creating a culture of service through people and practices and 3) bringing a business-perspective to factors that affect economic development.

The outline is simple enough. Not simple at all is doing justice to the incredibly complex issues, detailed analysis, and measures and methods required to transform each function into a working model of optimum performance. Three task forces – procurement, customer service and workforce development – receive special attention as examples of innovation, of influence and of impact on Georgia's future.

It took all of these efforts going in 24 different directions to pull together a major transformation of the way state government does business.

I. MANAGING THE ENTERPRISE FOR VALUE AND ACCOUNTABILITY

II. CREATING A CULTURE OF PERFORMANCE AND PUBLIC SERVICE

III. BUILDING THE ECONOMY WITH A BUSINESS PLAN

*"In many ways, our state was stuck in the 1990s,
80s and even 70s, bogged in outmoded ways
of business and ineffective growth strategies.
If we do this right, Georgia will turn a corner
in the management of government operations.
Around the corner is the 21ˢᵗ Century."*

LONICE BARRETT, DIRECTOR OF IMPLEMENTATION, 2004-2006

I. MANAGING THE ENTERPRISE FOR VALUE AND ACCOUNTABILITY

*"We are identifying the hidden costs of government – the inefficient ways we
do business and the negligent handling of our assets. We must hold ourselves
accountable."*

GOVERNOR SONNY PERDUE

The Governor's charge to the Commission was to examine the business
operations of government as if it were their own enterprise.

For some task forces, the assignment called for inspecting the underbelly of
the operational infrastructure and the boiler rooms of its workings. Their job
was to identify failing business models and broken processes.

For others, it was forensic accounting of fiscal and asset management. They
were not after fraud, but wrong-way practices that forfeited value of the state's
cash and real assets.

The task forces' groundwork of assessing existing operations revealed deep
dysfunctions, which led to recommended remedies and reforms, ranging

from re-engineering processes to converting to brand new business models.

In looking at business operations across the breadth of nearly a dozen management areas, the task forces found the state lacking effective organization, accountability and best practices in basic management functions.

The cost of government rises and falls on these factors, disregarded at great expense:

- *Assets*. The purchasing, usage and disposal of state assets based on their value, lifecycle and cost-of-ownership

- *Finance*. Cash flow practices, managing debt and obligations, and accounting oversight

- *Cost-drivers*. Trend-line indicators, process efficiency, controllable risk

- *Business practices*. Innovation, performance metrics, best practices

It was clear that operations had not moved with the times in advancing strategies and skills required to meet performance standards. Showing the way forward for the bureaucracy's migration to 21st Century business thinking was the Commission's strategic role.

Remember, a core principle in Commission thinking and recommendations was the concept of a government enterprise with common internal functions centralized in divisions to provide shared services. Center-led administrative support served three effective purposes:

- to keep statutory policies consistent and coordinated and across all agencies;

- to enforce accountability for reporting data and compliance with regulations;

- to let agencies do their assigned jobs instead of dealing with back-office administrative tasks which took expertise and resources they didn't possess.

The functions were as various as negotiating real estate leases, managing bank accounts, contracting vehicle maintenance, job classification and computer services.

The conversation about center-led, shared services started in earnest with the Administrative Services Task Force, which looked at the holistic picture of government-to-government operations from an enterprise perspective. (The work of the Administrative Services task force is detailed in Chapter 3). It was

TASK FORCE CATEGORIES

I. MANAGING THE ENTERPRISE FOR VALUE	II. CREATING A CULTURE OF SERVICE	III. BUILDING THE ECONOMY WITH A BUSINESS PLAN
ADMINISTRATIVE SERVICES	LEADERSHIP DEVELOPMENT	STRATEGIC INDUSTRIES
SPACE MANAGEMENT FLEET MGT. I & II	COMMUNITY CARE BEHAVIORAL HEALTH & DEVELOPMENTAL DISABILITIES	TOURISM
CAPITAL CONSTRUCTION		COMPETITIVENESS
	SERVICE DELIVERY	TRANSPORTATION
RECEIVABLES		FREIGHT & LOGISTICS
PUBLIC FINANCE OPTIONS	RECRUITMENT, RETENTION & RETIREMENT	COMMERCIALIZATION/ INTELLECTUAL PROPERTY
STATE HEALTH BENEFITS	*TASK FORCE FOCUS* CUSTOMER SERVICE	*TASK FORCE FOCUS*
AVIATION		WORKFORCE DEVELOPMENT
RISK MANAGEMENT		
STATE INVESTMENT STRATEGIES		
TASK FORCE FOCUS PROCUREMENT		

To provide the back story and detail of change initiatives and outcomes, the Commission for A New Georgia will maintain its existing website at *www.newgeorgia.org* through 2011 as a public repository of all reports and results of CNG and implementation initiatives.

clearly the "mother of all task forces" by virtue of its progeny – procurement, fleet management, space and construction, human resources, state health benefits and customer service.

The task force drew a new map for organizing internal services. Functions were realigned, pulling fragmented responsibilities and conflicting authority from scattered agencies and putting them together into coherent clusters under lead agencies. Their template became the foundation of the enterprise transformation.

The implementers took it from there, working the project through the feasibility check, the methodology to achieve a set of changes, and the empowerment for execution – legislation, executive orders, resources and a lead agency. Implementation Director Jeff Strane called these the "critical mass of elements to be effective."

"The task forces were really about determining the 'why' of change, and describing from a private-sector view the 'what' to do," Strane explained. "Implementation did the 'who' and 'how' – the personnel, organizational and structural elements that needed to be realigned and repositioned to create a comprehensive program."

Standing up a new business model can take months and years of getting everything right – the proposal, the funding, the technology, the process, the people – in incremental steps. It doesn't happen in a paragraph and a handful of bullets, except in books.

The following summaries encapsulate the issues, actions and results of each task force.

ADMINISTRATIVE SERVICES | 2004
CHAIR: JIM COPELAND
CONSULTING PARTNER: NORTH HIGHLAND

The task force evaluated the state's administrative operations. It focused on the agencies and departments that provide enterprise-wide services and support: procurement, state technology services, human resources, and management of state property and capital assets.

Of utmost concern was the fragmented administration of government-wide operations creating overlap, conflict and duplication. Their overarching recommendation was to align responsibilities for administrative services by function to promote clear policy-making, stronger accountability and customer focus.

The report led to the Commission's formation of specialized task forces to follow-up with comprehensive studies and recommendations in each of the administrative areas.

SPACE MANAGEMENT | 2004
CHAIR: LARRY GELLERSTEDT
CONSULTING PARTNER: IBM

State government is the biggest landlord of owned and leased real estate in Georgia and the nation's second biggest spender in consolidated funding of public construction. Four prior commissions have recommended getting control of the state's space consumption, which was managed by multiple agencies.

The task force found significant vacancies in both state buildings and leased space. Leasing rates were often above market, and offices were being rented in proximity to state buildings with vacant space. Some buildings were so deteriorated that the task force determined it was cheaper to demolish and rebuild rather than renovate. The report stated that "the state's investment in current space is losing value due to poor maintenance, safety issues and underutilization." The task force called for sweeping changes in the way the state manages its $11 billion investment in property. Every recommendation was implemented.

For the first time in Georgia's history, the long-sought goal of bringing all of the state's capital assets under a unified management system was a done deal.

RESULTS

- Governor Perdue appointed Georgia's first State Property Officer (SPO) to manage real estate as a total portfolio. Senate Bill 158 established the State Properties Commission to consolidate authority under the SPO. The portfolio is managed with a business approach focused on increasing the value of the assets through improving space utilization and minimizing occupancy costs.

- Georgia conducted the first state inventory of government-owned and -leased buildings and parcels of land to determine a total record of space, location, usage, value and cost of ownership. Georgia now has a comprehensive inventory on a GIS-based website where a catalog of all 15,000 buildings, 1,700 leases and 1.1 million acres is accessible to the public.

- Surplus property sales generated $43 million. Over 1,000 individual leases were consolidated and renegotiated, realizing $10 million in cumulative savings and cost avoidance. Colocating clusters of state offices in communities resulted in more cost-effective leases and a one-stop shop for citizens.

FLEET MANAGEMENT I & II | 2004
CHAIR I: ALBERT WRIGHT
CONSULTING PARTNER: AGL
CHAIR II: DON BURDESHAW
CONSULTING PARTNER: BEARING POINT

Agencies had amassed the nation's second largest fleet of state-owned passenger vehicles, a ratio of one for every five employees. Purchases and record-keeping were handled in-house. Personal vehicle assignments and commuting miles were many times higher than comparable states. Seven studies since the 1970s had recommended centralizing fleet management to reduce cars and costs and increase accountability.

Two task forces concurred with previous recommendations. They prescribed an inventory and agency audit to determine need, usage and operating cost of vehicles, followed by implementation of a statewide fleet management system.

RESULTS

- By Governor's orders, a complete inventory counted 21,419 vehicles. Nearly 1,900 vehicles were auctioned, generating $2.9 million and reducing costs by $4.3 million. The Capitol Hill motor pool was outsourced to Enterprise Rent-a-Car, eliminating 165 vehicles. Enterprise was also contracted to run a statewide rental pool as an option for agencies, saving millions in the cost of replacing and maintaining aging vehicles.

- In 2005, House Bill 312 strengthened centralized policy leadership for the fleet.

- The Office of Fleet Management (OFM) hired the director who made Utah a national model. OFM updated the policy and operations manual for the first time in 22 years.

- A Fleet Management System was purchased by Georgia in 1998, but only half of its 25,000 licenses were in effect. An updated system was implemented, creating a statewide repository for data on vehicles, maintenance mileage, purchases and disposal proceeds.

- An outsourced fuel service network was instituted to monitor consumption at the pump and catch reporting errors and fraud.

- Centralized contracting for maintenance saved agencies $555,335 in repair costs in one year. Scorecards were generated for each agency to show cost-effective options based on the agency's business needs for vehicles, and a trip calculator was provided to figure the cheapest mode of employee travel.

CAPITAL CONSTRUCTION | 2004
CHAIR: JIM CARSON
CONSULTING PARTNER: ACCENTURE

The Capital Construction Task Force found that in addition to the problems with existing buildings, Georgia was spending $700 million to $1 billion a year to construct even more buildings under equally disordered conditions.

The task force examined the strategy and processes by which the state finances, designs, builds and maintains its capital construction projects. Among the issues considered were the efficiency of project management and factors that drive up the cost of construction. Task force recommendations were integrated into the total management approach under the State Property Officer.

RESULTS

- In 2007, a new Statewide Construction Manual became the first end-to-end guide on how to conduct a state capital construction project – a process that hadn't been updated since 1954.

- State capital project managers have closed in on a goal of 100 percent on-time/on-budget completion. Less than half the projects met those goals prior to 2007.

- The task force found that more than $80 million in bonds were obligated to canceled projects. A policy was implemented to manage bond proceeds on a milestone basis to identify undeveloped projects.

ACCOUNTS RECEIVABLE | 2005
CHAIR: DONNA HYLAND
CONSULTING PARTNER: KPMG

Since 2008, several billion dollars in state revenue has dried up in the dust-bowl of the Great Recession. Meanwhile, an estimated $5 billion in unpaid bills are owed to the state from seriously delinquent taxes, fees, reimbursements and federal grants.

The task force studied a sample of 10 agencies with combined budgets of

$5 billion, representing about 30 percent of the state budget. Together these agencies showed overdue accounts exceeding $1 billion. Federal grants were $68 million in arrears. Agencies had no state policy direction for collecting debts.

The task force recommended establishing a central State Accounting Office to get a handle on all financial reporting, including receivable accounts and cash flow. They also put a priority on collecting high-dollar debts and consolidating hundreds of agency bank accounts to manage cash to better advantage.

RESULTS

- In 2005, House Bill 293 created Georgia's first State Accounting Officer to realign financial reporting and financial systems in one office.

- In 2006, statewide accounting standards were implemented, and Georgia met the deadline for the Consolidated Annual Financial Report for the first time since 1991.

- The Department of Revenue recovered more than $570 million in receivables from 2004-2009 using a surge of new, aggressive tactics, including posting delinquent taxpayer's names online, garnishing IRS refunds, and withholding alcohol and auto dealer licenses until past due taxes are paid.

- The project to streamline banking reduced the number of agency accounts by more that 50 percent, saving service fees and increasing interest rates.

PUBLIC FINANCE OPTIONS | 2005
CHAIR: PHIL HUMANN
CONSULTING PARTNER: GOLDMAN-SACHS

The good news in 2004, even in the uncertainty of recession, was Georgia's firm position as one of seven states earning the fiscal gold-standard of a AAA bond rating. But Georgia's booming population was overrunning roads, schools and water resources, confronting the state with massive capital project needs to be financed by borrowing.

Georgia's Constitution was ironclad with restrictions to debt levels, length of bond terms and other safeguards against over-borrowing. The task force looked at possible alternatives to finance capital projects and focused on financial management measures to protect the golden bond rating.

RESULTS

- House Bill 509 doubled the maximum level of the Revenue Shortfall Reserve from five percent of prior year's revenues to 10 percent.

- A debt management plan created a dynamic model that allowed the finance team to evaluate and measure appropriate levels of debt for the state.

- Multi-year financial and capital planning were adopted.

- Financial planning systems were upgraded on PeopleSoft to deliver timely financial reports, a factor in credit ratings.

STATE HEALTH BENEFITS PLAN | 2005
CO-CHAIRS: BILL WALLACE
ELLEN LINDEMANN
CONSULTING PARTNER: HEWITT ASSOCIATES

Like the nation, Georgia was hurting badly from the cost of healthcare. Rocketing insurance payouts for 650,000 state employees, dependents and retirees were overshooting the state's trust fund by $300 million and were soaring annually by double-digits. Premium increases had pushed the plan to the edge of affordability for low-wage employees and retirees.

The task force recommendations focused on cost containment by balancing health coverage with fiscal responsibility on the consumer side. They also took into account that health insurance is a major factor in recruiting and retaining the best employees.

RESULTS

- An expanded consumer-driven health plan was developed, with premium pricing to spur enrollment.

- Tiered coverage created more pricing options for dependent care.

- Coordination with Medicare reduced the cost of covering retirees.

- Plans and administration were streamlined to offer a lower-cost network option.

- Surcharges were applied to smokers and to spouses covered by other plans, and wellness credits were enhanced.

AVIATION | 2006
CHAIR: RANDY HUDON

Over and above vehicles, the state owns a "flying fleet" – propeller planes, jets and helicopters covering the gamut of air missions, from law enforcement to transporting state officials.

As the years went by, agencies began acquiring their own air assets. Eventually there were "four little air forces" flying 85 planes and copters. The fleet was a hodgepodge of a dozen different models of aircraft. Over half were older than 20 years, including surplus from Vietnam. Training, maintenance and safety were up to agencies, which hired their own mechanics and pilots by their own standards. When business was slow, pilots were idle.

A task force of experienced professional aviation managers and pilots reported deficiencies in aviation practices and standards on top of high operating costs. They recommended consolidating aviation services in one authority which would cross-utilize aircraft and pilots to cover all missions with fewer assets. Fleet modernization would reduce the cost of maintenance and increase safety.

RESULTS

- In 2009, Senate Bill 85 established the Georgia Aviation Authority, consolidating state-owned air assets in a single aviation service for all missions under one command. A seasoned aviation manager and pilot with both corporate and Coast Guard command experience became the first executive director.

- Pilots have been certified for deployment on any mission.

- Surplus aircraft have gone on the auction block. The plan is to further reduce the working fleet to 36. Hangar closings will reduce bases to 10, strategically located around the state.

RISK MANAGEMENT | 2006
CHAIR: PROFESSOR LARRY GAUNT

More than $100 million a year is spent "by accident" on state vehicle collisions, workplace injuries, property damage and liability claims. The state's risk exposure encompasses 130,000 employees, nearly 20,000 vehicles and $27 billion in property. That makes Georgia's insurance program comparable to the largest corporations in the U.S.

The task force found that despite the magnitude of its business, the Risk Management Services Division didn't operate by accepted industry standards and lacked professional personnel. They recommended reorganizing RMS and hiring certified managers to implement practices that minimize the cost of risk and better manage claims.

RESULTS

- RMS on-boarded an experienced insurance professional as director and added qualified loss-control officers and IT staff. Their goals went beyond better-business practices to pro-active measures, creating a "culture of safety."

- Senate Bill 425 expanded RMS authority to charge the cost of premiums to agencies based on their record of claims. Tying premiums to performance incentivizes agencies to work aggressively on controlling causes of high-loss liability. Performance measures have been established for agencies to gauge and reduce their risk.

- A Comprehensive Loss Control Program has been implemented. In its first year, claims were down nine percent – 1,100 fewer cases. Payout costs dived 6.5 percent, saving $6 million. Property claims were reduced by 31 percent through an aggressive building-and-grounds inspection program.

- RMS has partnered with the Attorney General's office to negotiate settlements and avoid multi-million dollar trials when the state is known to be at fault.

- In a single year, greater scrutiny of worker's compensation claims and billing resulted in savings of nearly $31 million.

STATE INVESTMENT STRATEGIES | 2009
CHAIR: WENDELL STARKE

Georgia's separate state employee and teacher pension funds, totaling about $55 billion, are managed by the Division of Investment Services (DIS) in line with the state's overall conservative approach to risking capital. In recent years a gap was widening between the state's conservative investment returns and its liberal benefits payout. A big bill was about to come due as the Boomer generation began to collect retirement checks. Georgia was the only state which still restricted investments in alternative categories of more aggressive funds, such as venture capital, infrastructure and private equity.

The task force found that although the total fund performed extremely well within its legal limitations, returns trailed comparable funds for the decade. They recommended the state expand options that would enhance returns without defying prudence.

RESULTS

- House Bill 371 liberalized asset allocations, allowing pension funds to increase investments in equities incrementally up to 75 percent. Venture capital was off the table.

- An external review was ordered on a three-to-five year cycle to monitor the performance of Georgia's funds vis-à-vis the larger fund universe.

PROCUREMENT | 2004
CHAIR: JIM BALLOUN

"I would say everyone was doing their best. We didn't find any fraud or corruption. It was just a large fragmented system where everyone was working hard and buying a lot of stuff."

TASK FORCE CHAIR JIM BALLOUN

Procurement was the number one case on the Commission's docket. As a business process, it was the largest source of both spending and potential cost savings in the bureaucracy. Purchase orders surpassed $5 billion a year for the "stuff" it takes to run the government – not even counting all school systems and universities.

The 2004 Procurement Task Force reviewed seven government studies done in the previous 10 years which took serious issue with Georgia's purchasing practices.

The way purchasing was done in 2004 was a quasi free-for-all. Agencies largely operated their own procurement shops, circumventing as much as possible the Department of Administrative Services' (DOAS) State Purchasing Department (SPD). The Commission's Administrative Services Task Force had noted in its earlier report that the SPD's cumbersome processes to author, release, evaluate and award large contracts took six-to-nine months.

The Procurement Task Force consultants from McKinsey interviewed about 40 staff and stakeholders caught in the procurement web. A sample of what they heard told the story on the ground:

"It's usually an administrative bidding exercise with little value added."

"I don't have the people who can do what I know is required."

"I couldn't tell you what we spend with whom."

"We just don't have the time and resources to understand supplier markets."

"I wish everyone would stop coding everything as 999 (other)."

Nevertheless, the team learned that agencies were willing to work with DOAS if they could count on effectiveness, speed and accuracy.

In 2004, the task force produced an 87-page analysis of needs and steps to bring state purchasing technologies and tactics into the 21st Century.

Their report arrived with the bodacious title "World Class Procurement for Georgia." The task force outlined a transformation process of seven phases, beginning with establishment of a center-leading procurement agency and ending with the launch of a statewide business model for procurement. Transitioning from the beginning to the end would require intensive up-grading of processes, staff skills, performance management and technology, plus legislation to centralize purchasing.

The task force agreed that a modernized, centralized system could save in the range of $100 million annually.

In 2005, Senate Bill 312 authorized a center-led procurement function, and the appropriations bill included $20 million to fund the transformation.

An experienced procurement professional with private-sector experience was brought in to honcho the transformation and was later appointed DOAS commissioner. Brad Douglas found he'd stepped into a procurement time warp, circa mid-1970s. He had virtually no meaningful data to assess. Purchasing agents didn't keep records of their suppliers and contracts, so his department couldn't review transactions by the 120 agencies and 35 state universities that spend state money. The last audit was done in 1991.

"They didn't read it, they didn't look at it, they didn't analyze it," Douglas said of bids for goods. "The bid price had no bearing on what the price could have been or should have been."

The bulk of the legislative funding was spent to contract A.T. Kearney (ATK) to bring in the expertise and people-power to manage the transformation project. They estimated it would take three years to build a new system from the bottom up and launch it statewide. To start, ATK literally hand counted purchase orders to extract spending data and aggregate the major categories of commodities bought by agencies.

In the next five years, the purchasing system made a 30-year leap forward, from paper-pushing processes to an electronic "marketplace." Strategically-sourced contracts leveraged the state's buying power to drive down prices. Category experts focused on the real value of purchases – taking into account maintenance cost, fit with current systems and age of the technology – to ensure items would work and last. Their analyses transformed the process from transaction-based to knowledge-based.

Streamlined processes cut four-to-six weeks off the request process to start the bidding. Vendors who challenge awards get resolution in two weeks instead of two months – but challenges are now rare.

In 2009, the eProcurement platform, known as Team Georgia Marketplace, changed everything about the way agencies shop for goods and services. It spread the market to new vendors and products in on-line catalogs, which shortened cycle times in a paperless process. In the first year, over $1 billion in purchases were processed through the system, providing valuable insight into what is being purchased by state agencies.

Georgia's procurement operation is gaining a national reputation as a leader and innovator of best practices.

In 2009, the Pew Center on the States selected Georgia's innovative work on a comprehensive spending analytics model as a Lab State Project and awarded funding and technical assistance to expedite the development. Georgia's "spend cube" will be shared with other states through Pew's network. The applied technology fills a major gap in collecting and analyzing spending information from all sources – including, for the first time, the 35 campuses of the University System – to put together all the pieces of the spending puzzle. The information can be viewed from multiple aspects – by category, by vendor, by purchaser – and by deep dives into the itemized purchases by an office. The system works across the disparate purchasing sources, from supplier data and PeopleSoft to agency procurement cards.

The combination of strategic sourcing and spending analytics has cut pricing for major categories of commodities by double digits. Here are a few examples of savings in commonly-purchased state goods and services:

- A new contract lowers pricing for copying and printing – up to 42 percent for black and white and as much as 87 percent for color.

- Outsourcing the Capitol Hill motor pool has eliminated 160 state-owned vehicles and has dropped rental rates by 14 percent.

- During a time when spiking petroleum and chemical prices were driving up the market cost of paint by 36 percent, Georgia negotiated discounts of 50-60 percent for paints, thinners and varnishes used to maintain state buildings.

- Statewide contracts purchase police-pursuit vehicles almost 16 percent below dealer invoice, and agency cars, sedans, vans and pick-ups average 22 percent below invoice.

As told in an earlier chapter, Procurement Task Force Chair Jim Balloun had both spurred and spearheaded the Commission's initiative to take on the state's broken purchasing system, based on his company's experience in converting to e-procurement. It was an example, he said, of the willingness of the business community to share their knowledge and experience with government to get better results for taxpayers.

"Just the Governor's act of setting up the Commission, asking for help and saying he was interested in learning, brought forth ideas," he said. "My great hope is the next governor will understand it is not just an accident that all this happened."

LANDMARKS OF MANAGING FOR ACCOUNTABILITY

ASSET MANAGEMENT

HB 158 - Historical achievement of consolidating all real property and construction under a unified management system

- First State Property Officer
- First comprehensive public database of all state buildings, lands and leases
- Total Cost-of-Ownership approach to space utilization, including lease consolidation, co-location, maintenance, energy management

HB 312 - Center-led Management of Fleet and Surplus Property

- First state inventory of vehicles
- System accountable for managing fleet across the lifecycle
- Cost-saving contracts for purchasing, maintenance, fuel
- Outsourcing and cost-effective options for agency travel

SB 85 - Georgia Aviation Authority

- First on-time Consolidated Annual Financial Report in 15 years
- Streamlined banking and cash management governed by uniform accounting standards and systems
- Aggressive, systematic collections process for delinquent accounts

FINANCIAL MANAGEMENT AND COST DRIVERS

HB 293 - First State Accounting Officer

- First on-time Consolidated Annual Financial Report in 15 years

- Streamlined banking and cash management governed by uniform accounting standards and systems

- Aggressive, systematic collections process for delinquent accounts

HB 509 - Revenue Shortfall Reserve

HB 371 - Liberalized Retirement Fund Investment

State Health Benefits

- Streamlined administration, menu of plans and prescription coverage

- Cost-containment measures, including shifts to Medicare coverage

- Consumer responsibility for choices

21ˢᵀ CENTURY BEST-BUSINESS PRACTICES

HB 312 - First State Accounting Officer

- Procurement Transformation from paper-pusher to strategic buyer to a national leader and innovator

SB 425 - Risk Management Services – authority to adjust agency premiums by loss

- Pro-active risk management and first Comprehensive Cost-Loss Program to reduce claims

II. CREATING A CULTURE OF PERFORMANCE AND PUBLIC SERVICE

"It's my experience that in any organization, you'll find 20 percent of the employees are passionate about what they do and 20 percent are on the other end, the whiners. The battle is for the 60 percent in between. Who are they going to listen to?"

JOE DOYLE, ADMINISTRATOR OF CONSUMER AFFAIRS AND CUSTOMER SERVICE

Where many citizens see "nameless, faceless bureaucrats," Joe Doyle sees "hearts and minds." For four years his mission has been about winning the heart-mind battle for culture change, freeing employees from old notions of government work and taking them to a new mindset of public service.

"What I saw were talented people who were not trusted, respected or empowered to do common sense things," Doyle said. "If we keep them

TECHNOLOGY TRANSFORMATION:
THE EX-OFFICIO TASK FORCE

CHAIR: PATRICK MOORE
EXECUTIVE DIRECTOR, GEORGIA TECHNOLOGY AUTHORITY, AND STATE CHIEF
INFORMATION OFFICER

Anyone whose job is tied to life-support on a networked computer knows from frightening experience that a hiccup in the system can hobble an entire project or office. Multiply that across 70,000 state employees, 1,400 state and local government departments and every major function in the state bureaucracy, and the implications of a shaky IT infrastructure teeter on catastrophic.

That was the condition of technology systems which ran the major operations of the State of Georgia until 2009. PCs too old to support anti-virus software were vulnerable to attack. Service was regularly interrupted by power failures in critical IT systems. Broken servers failed to backup important data.

Within a week in office in January 2003, Governor Perdue appointed his administration's first task force. Their assignment was to recommend a path to a technology system that could reliably meet government's growing dependence on computing services and telecommunications. Security was a primary issue, magnified by the increasing ingenuity of hackers.

The task force recommendations were presented at the first meeting of the Commission for A New Georgia. Later, the Commission's own task force on Administrative Services recommended the Georgia Technology Authority (GTA) refocus on its core mission to develop and promote IT planning, policies, processes and services for state agencies.

In reality, the state could not compete with the know-how of the giants of technology in the private sector when it came to providing IT systems with the power to support the state enterprise. In 2007, the Georgia Technology Authority undertook one of the largest public-sector technology transformations in the world, valued at $1.2 billion over 10 years and affecting every major function in the state, school systems and local governments. In 2009, IT infrastructure services were turned over to IBM and managed network services to AT&T. GTA was downsized from 600 employees to about 170 and shifted its focus to managing the delivery of services. The business model projects savings of $203 million over the life of the IBM and AT&T contracts.

In terms of Commission initiated-transformations, the capability to provide powerful, reliable, sophisticated technologies is the backbone of new systems across the enterprise: customer service call centers, driver services identification checks, human resources networking and asset management databases.

It is indeed the lifeline of a best-managed state.

in situations where they are doomed to fail, we cannot ask that person to change their behavior."

Business processes and systems change the mechanics of how government works, transitioning to tools that amp up performance. Culture is the softer side of transformation, but harder to install – no heart/brain transplants to jumpstart new standards of service.

In Governor Perdue's thinking, people and processes are inextricably linked in the value proposition for service delivery. It was a concept readily grasped by the business executives on Commission for A New Georgia as key to Georgia's Best-Managed State aspirations. The Commission viewed culture change across the broad horizon of the enterprise and selected areas where task forces could launch initiatives with impact:

- *Customer Service.* Faster, friendlier, easier services for the public through better customer relations, more efficient processes and effective telephone assistance.

- *Human Resources.* Recruiting and retaining high-caliber employees and creating the environment of a "Best Place to Work" throughout state government.

- *Leadership Development.* Preparing administrators for an expanded role as executives and creating a pipeline of talented, trained leaders for state service.

- *Service Delivery.* Ensuring equity and quality of state services in all of Georgia's regions.

- *Community Care for Behavioral Health and Development Disorders.* Zeroing in on an identified problem affecting critical services to nearly 400,000 Georgians at the community level, a case study in system failure.

The success stories of cultural change take place at the most human level and on both sides of the government exchange – the employee and the taxpaying customer – putting a smiley face on the "faceless" bureaucracy.

LEADERSHIP DEVELOPMENT | 2004
CHAIR: LEE LEE JAMES
CONSULTING PARTNER: CARL VINSON INSTITUTE OF GOVERNMENT

State government's effectiveness in continuously improving efficiency of operations and service is directly related to the quality of leadership in departments and agencies.

As government prepares for an exodus of seasoned administrators – 21% are eligible to retire before the end of the decade – the task force looked at the state's strategy and procedures for identifying and training leaders of the future.

RESULTS

- In August 2005, the Governor's Office established the Georgia Leadership Institute (GLI), the first succession-planning function in state government.

- The institute builds leadership throughout state employees' careers and creates a pipeline of talent at supervisory, managerial and executive levels. The program is delivered statewide through the UGA-Carl Vinson Institute of Government.

- As of 2009, GLI had graduated 384 employees in the Executive Leadership Program, 110 in middle management and 142 in front-line leadership. Approximately 9,000 employees have been trained in the workforce development programs.

- The Executive Leadership Development Program (ELDP) was instituted as a one-of-a kind program targeting prospects for agencies' top positions. The course capstone is a challenge project addressing an actual issue in the participant's agency.

COMMUNITY CARE for BEHAVIORAL HEALTH AND DEVELOPMENTAL DISABILITIES | 2005
CHAIR: BRUCE COOK

State agencies estimate that around 300,000 of the people served by schools, family services and prisons are struggling with diagnosed mental, behavioral or developmental problems. Two state audits of the Community Service Board (CSB) delivery system concluded that its complexity was overwhelming for clients, pushing many to state hospitals when they could be treated in their communities at less cost.

The task force found a direly disordered system. CSB-funding was based on historical patterns, not current populations or need, and providers set their own overhead and rates with widely varying costs. Lack of intervention for released inmates with drug and mental problems led to a revolving door of re-incarceration. Troubled youth bounced around a disconnected social services system in schools, juvenile court and family programs.

This was the first task force to go public, conducting public hearings and meetings with agencies and service providers. Recommendations identified best practices and specific steps in a systematic transformation to eliminate disparities in mental health services and provide access to intervention.

RESULTS

- In 2009, House Bill 228 established the Department of Behavioral Health and Developmental Disabilities (DBHDD) as a stand-alone agency for mental health, developmental disabilities and addictive disease. It created a coordinating council involving departments of Family and Children Services, Juvenile Justice, and Community Health to move to a single system of care.

- System-of-care approaches have systematically engaged schools and other child services with the parents of troubled children.

- The wraparound approach to care has been extended to youth with severe emotional disorders who do not meet criteria for residential treatment but need intensive services.

RECRUITMENT, RETENTION, RETIREMENT | 2006
CHAIR: BILL WALLACE
CONSULTING PARTNER: HEWITT

The Administrative Services Task Force described the management of human resources as a sore spot of "highly inefficient" functions. Agencies had doubled the number of HR staff in the state to a ratio well above the national average, building in-house personnel shops and proliferating job classifications to over 3,500 titles.

In a workforce of nearly 130,000, half had been on the job less than six years, and turnover was 37 percent among first-year employees. The state benefits package was over market in retirement and low on pay scales required to attract quality applicants.

In 2006, a new commissioner was hired from corporate management to head the state personnel agency. His goals were to upgrade workforce quality, unify HR policies and practices, and brand state government as an Employer of Choice.

"We had to get away from the mentality that we're just a state, that we've got entitlement programs and that we're not interested in recruiting the best people because we don't have the money to pay them," said State Personnel Commissioner Steve Stevenson. "We want the best people doing work for the citizens of Georgia."

The task force viewed the span of the HR lifecycle, including incentives to recruit and retain the best employees and updating retirement plans to fit the mobility of the emerging generation of employee prospects. Recommendations echoed the call to centralize human resources. Under this system, the state acts as a single employer in job classification, policy and services, while allowing agencies flexibility in hiring and managing personnel.

RESULTS

- Senate Bill 230 gave the State Personnel Administration (SPA) authority to set HR policy and best practices for all state employees. Shared services cut administrative costs and reduced transaction errors, with estimated 2010 savings of $522,000.

- A new-hire retirement plan combined traditional benefits and 401Ks with a state match. Redesigned jobs and pay-for-performance upped the ante in competing for talented applicants.

- The State's 3,500 jobs classifications were consolidated to 750. Restructured pay scales more fairly compensated employees with similar responsibilities.

- In 2008, Careers.ga.gov opened a portal to state employment opportunities and launched an aggressive marketing campaign that won a national award for online recruitment videos.

SERVICE DELIVERY | 2007
CHAIR: PAUL WOOD
CONSULTING PARTNER: CARL VINSON INSTITUTE OF GOVERNMENT

The long and winding road from state government services to customers at the community level passes through layers of government and crosses boundaries of different districts for different services.

The task force looked at Georgia's system for regional planning districts, which had been around for 50 years under various names and geographical districts. Over time, regions became increasingly unequal in population, funding and service. Districts were as small as 100,000 and as large as 600,000. Rural areas were most impacted by low per capita funding and poorly performing RDCs.

Recommendations focused on redistricting and creating new Regional Commissions (RC) with uniform governance, funding and accountability.

RESULTS

- House Bill 1216, passed in 2008, changed the boundaries and reduced the number of districts from 16 to 12 to create a critical mass of constituents and funding. Commission boards appointed by the Governor, Lieutenant

Governor and Speaker of the House established equity and gave the state a voice in each region.

- The Department of Audits and Accounts was ordered to review the level of services and finances in all districts on a three-year rotation.

- In 2010, House Bill 867 established an oversight Commission on Regional Planning chaired by the Governor and the state's top elected officials. The board created a forum for improving efficiency, reducing costs and strengthening state-level accountability.

TASK FORCE FOCUS

CUSTOMER SERVICE | 2005
CHAIR: JOE DOYLE

"We turned to the employees and showed them how to fix their own problems. They saw management was listening to them, what they were suggesting was getting done, and the results were better for the customer. So employees are now beaming with pride and accomplishment."

JOE DOYLE, ADMINISTRATOR OF CONSUMER AFFAIRS AND CUSTOMER SERVICE

State government is perceived by most citizens most of the time as that reputed "nameless, faceless bureaucracy." But when a close encounter with a state office turns into hours in line, or 20 minutes holding the phone, or months to process a routine transaction, government gets personal. The impression made by that office sticks the whole government with the label of lousy service.

Joe Doyle spent 30 years running his own national retail chain before he arrived in state government as a newbie administrator in 2004. One day he had his turn on the customer side of the counter in a local drivers license bureau. After 45 minutes in line, he was greeted by this sign: "If you are here to renew your license, you do not need to be in this line." Who knew?

That was standard service across many agencies. Parents were stranded for three months waiting for child support orders to be processed. Callers to state agencies and information centers were left in hold-the-phone eternity – 56 minutes in one case on record. Of an estimated 50 million calls to government every year, more than half were answered by a machine, and millions were abandoned or misdirected. Back at the license bureaus, driver tests were backlogged 16 weeks, offices closed for lunch while people were in line, and anyone who didn't present exact cash for the fee was turned away – no checks or credit cards.

Governor Perdue had already decided to do something about extricating the license process from the tangle of law enforcement and commercial transactions in the Department of Motor Vehicles. But what about the other 2,000 services provided by 138,000 employees in state government?

In 2005, that was the challenge charged to the Commission's Customer Service Task Force, headed by Doyle. Unlike other task forces, he worked with an inside-government team. That notwithstanding, the product was to be a business case for substantive change, he said, "not slogans and tee-shirts."

The task force data from surveys and service metrics agreed with the typical complaints about government services: hard to contact, long lines, slow processes, unresponsive, and sometimes plain unfriendly. Service mapping showed that some processes went from desk to desk, handled by different people, so a three-month process may only involve three hours of actual attention. That was the case in getting child support orders to court.

The task force recommended three major components of a total overhaul of the state's customer service culture.

1. Start creating the culture and setting expectations for how the state should serve customers – the "hearts and minds" piece. The idea was to adopt broad service standards spearheaded by a state coordinator and implemented by champions in each agency. Best practices for training, recognition and rewards were built into the program.

2. Adopt a Rapid Process Improvement methodology to speed up service in customer-intensive departments with low satisfaction ratings. The plan would involve present personnel in problem-solving and driving expeditious improvement on a continuous basis.

3. Establish a general information service as a single point of access for state services through a 1-800 call center with live operators. An encyclopedia of services on a central database would be shared by all call handlers, including remote and outsourced operators. Upgrading technology and training across the board would provide seamless service for any caller.

"A focus on the customer keeps government in touch with its citizens and reinforces the goal of excellent service," the task force concluded. "The benefits of enhanced access to state agencies along with consistent communication and evaluation will enable Georgia to provide the best customer service of any state in the nation."

In January 2006, the Governor signed an executive order creating the nation's first state-wide customer service agency. He summoned 120 agency heads, key staff and exemplary employees to a two-day training summit to launch the initiative. Perdue announced that Doyle would lead the effort started by the task force he chaired.

It was also the debut of the Team Georgia standard for improving services: Faster, Friendlier, Easier. The mantra would soon spread across the state on banners and buttons. A regular mailing of e-postcards spotlighted employees in the act of providing exceptional service. Monthly newsletters of success stories kept a drumbeat going across the state.

Within agencies, designated champions promoted core values that apply to every employee regardless of job: be helpful, accessible, courteous, knowledgeable and responsive. Everyone was called to get creative in using their ready resources to take value up a notch. The key was getting better results with the same people. More than a smiley-face exercise, customer service performance was incorporated by the State Personnel Administration into the formal annual employee appraisal.

Doyle said employees "getting beat up hour by hour by angry customers" were equally frustrated by senseless processes they knew how to fix, if anyone would listen. Rapid Process Improvement teams and employee-led work groups collaborated on ways to apply a streamlined version of lean management to achieve improvement by reconfiguring the chain of actions in the process. The results could be amazing. Approval of Peachcare-for-Kids health coverage was shortcut from 113 days to 15 days. Mental health providers for severely stretched community-based programs were certified for service in 96 days instead of 18 months. Motor vehicle titles take five days to process, compared to the old standard of six weeks. Preparing child support orders for court can now be turned around in one day in all 159 counties. And Drivers Services Centers, which once averaged two-hour lines, can typically greet customers at the counter within six minutes. The metrics count. The Office of Planning and Budget requires agencies to show improvement outcomes in their annual budget requests.

On the call-center front, 1-800-georgia went live in January 2008. Trained operators answer and match information from the caller to a database of services and route the call to the right place on the first connection. The technology platform networked the centers, so they can share peak loads.

Customer service stories abound across the state, as 50 agencies and all 35 University System of Georgia campuses participate in the training, metrics and celebration. The Governor personally hands out annual awards for customer service to employees whose examples of extraordinary care for citizens bring tears to the audience.

Greg Dozier, who took on the re-engineering of the Department of Driver Services, watched the pride grow in his employees, who worked for an agency that was once so detested they were embarrassed to go to lunch in their DDS uniform shirt. Now they are smiling along with the customers.

In 2009, a series of public surveys rated the state's overall service quality at 76 percent – better than Wal-Mart's and just short of Nordstrom's. Employee satisfaction was 70 percent, up 10 points despite a no-raise year and furloughs.

"People always wanted to offer that service level, but that was not the focus in government," Dozier said. "When you have the new leader of the state come and in and say, 'I want service to match the citizen's expectations,' good government is redefined.

"I think we really lit a fire across state government. Those who had given their life's career in providing these services and had always wanted to see them be a focal point of quality suddenly had that opportunity."

LANDMARKS OF A CULTURE OF PERFORMANCE AND SERVICE

HUMAN RESOURCES

SB 230 – State Personnel Administration for HR policy and practices

- Center-led, shared administrative services across HR processes
- Job classifications restructured with commensurate, market-based pay
- Total rewards package revamped to attract the new generation of talent
- Pay for performance tied to state and agency goals
- State Government marketed as Employer of Choice for job options and benefits

Leadership Development

- First Georgia Leadership Institute for development of high-performers and succession-planning
- Continuous pipeline of talent at all levels of management
- Executive Leadership Development Program for top-level agency and executive prospects

CUSTOMER SERVICE

Nation's first enterprise-wide state government customer service program

- Rapid Process Improvement project managers and employee-led teams reinvent faster, friendlier, easier services
- Metrics validate improvements, customer satisfaction
- Customer service training and educational campaign reaching all employees
- 1-800 call center for one-source access connecting citizens with all state services

SERVICE DELIVERY

SB 1216 – Regional Commissions restructured service districts

- Reduced number of districts to equalize population and funding
- Established uniform membership, services and accountability reviews

SB 867 created oversight commission of top state executives

SB 230 – Department of Behavioral Health and Developmental Disabilities

- Moved to a single system of care, coordinating services across departments involved with mental disorders, addiction and troubled youth
- Hospitalizations reduced, community-care alternatives expanded
- Provider pool increased and required to meet accreditation standards
- Emphasis on crisis stabilization, employment support and recovery-based intervention
- Focus on programs and parental involvement to help youth with severe emotional disorders outside detention

III. BUILDING THE ECONOMY WITH A BUSINESS PLAN

"Absolutely, economic development is our top issue. We want to recruit more companies to Georgia, but we also want to facilitate the growth of start-ups. We want existing businesses to grow."

GOVERNOR SONNY PERDUE

The Commission for A New Georgia had been clearly established in the role of a business advisor, and the economy runs on business systems. The Commission's executives knew something about managing to succeed in a competitive market.

Seven task forces were called upon to evaluate the organization and business plans of economic development and drivers. They enlisted an array of resource people to bring to the tasks the sort of data, knowledge bases, best practices and innovative ideas that were used to improve performance in administrative and service areas.

Pulling out of recession in 2004, the early task forces were concerned foremost with growing back the economy. The job market was transitioning to the demand for a workforce more skilled than the labor pool laid off by Georgia's shuttered plants. Global competitors were taking jobs to the far side of the flat world.

One task force identified growth industries that would best fit Georgia's assets and recommended six categories as targets for development. A task force on competitiveness assessed the multiplicity of approaches used to market the state and sell corporate prospects on Georgia's assets. Their recommendation prescribed a more organized center-led effort with the Governor's Office out front.

The Commission also paid attention to existing industries which needed a shot of innovative thinking to recharge their potential. Tourism was singled out for its positives and negatives – it generated a huge number of dollars and jobs, but it was lagging the Southeast as a leader in visitor traffic. The task force proposed a public-private venture to start and sustain an aggressive marketing campaign.

Two task forces considered value-building opportunities – one to upgrade the competitiveness of Georgia's workforce and the other to raise the marketability of Georgia's research properties.

The Governor's Office of Workforce Development grew out of a task force's recommendations on unifying education, employment and economic planning as a force for building a skilled and marketable labor force. The timing was prescient. Before the 2008 recession, the WFD Office was on the job building certified, work-ready employment bases in communities to increase their competitiveness as a business location.

The state's vast repositories of intellectual properties and research talent in the sciences lacked visibility in the market that attracts commercial development and company creation. Georgia researchers were particularly productive in life-sciences discoveries, which put that field on the priority list of industries to recruit and develop. The Commission pushed for a single web-based portal for the state's public and private research universities to get Georgia's research products into the marketplace.

The physical infrastructure for expanding economic development drastically needed tending, particularly in transportation. While planners worked on the strategic map for highway expansion and routes, Commission task forces were scrutinizing two key factors that impact decisions. One task force dissected the process for contracting road projects to identify cost-saving strategies. Another task force was feeding in data on freight movement as a major user of the transportation network. Both task forces contributed vital pieces of process and planning to the larger transportation strategy.

The economic implosion that wrecked Georgia's once enviable employment rate and business growth magnifies the necessity and expectation for the state's government and private sector to work together to rebuild the future. The Commission's role of bringing smart management to state strategies and operations provided a prototype for meeting that challenge.

STRATEGIC INDUSTRIES | 2004
CHAIR: DAVE GARRETT
CONSULTING PARTNERS: DELOITTE, BOARD OF REGENTS, SPF GROUP, GEORGIA TECH

Across the nation, economic development priorities were transitioning to a world of new opportunities, competition and ways of bringing businesses and jobs to states. In the task force's assessment, Georgia's economic development efforts were unfocused, uncoordinated and reactive rather than proactive. "Our process becomes the prospect's problem," the report stated. Georgia's research and commercialization assets, they concluded, were not being leveraged to spur growth.

The task force recommended a unified economic development strategy led by the Governor's Office. Six strategic industries were identified as innovative, high-growth fields that could drive economic expansion for the long term and significantly raise the average wage for Georgians. The industries were aerospace, agribusiness, energy and environmental concerns, healthcare and eldercare, life sciences, and logistics and transportation. These industries were considered magnets for growth of supporting industries which could be spread throughout regions. The task force endorsed university research parks to increase commercialization of Georgia discoveries.

RESULTS

- Governor Perdue created Centers of Innovation (COI) to assist companies in each of the six strategic industry areas. Located around the state, the centers were based on the successful Georgia Electronic Design Center business model which exchanges access to "talent, ideas and equipment" in Georgia's research universities to job creation in the state. Each Center connects to a Research University in one of the State's strategic industries.

- The Department of Economic Development restructured its Global Commerce Division around five industry-focused teams and an international investment team to recruit prospects considering location in Georgia. The divisions align resources to court companies that have strategic value to the state.

- A Technology Enterprise Park was built adjacent to Georgia Tech in 2008. Initial tenants utilized the States Facility Fund program to secure and outfit labs.

- The Georgia Research Alliance developed the iResearch portal to university patents and scientists as a marketplace for companies to shop for patented properties and research with development potential.

TOURISM | 2004
CHAIR: PHIL JACOBS
CONSULTING PARTNERS: GEORGIA STATE UNIVERSITY,
GEORGIA TECH

More than 9,000 tourism-related businesses employ 200,000 Georgians and generate $16.1 billion for communities and the State. It's the one industry than can't be exported out of Georgia, but it is particularly vulnerable to recessions and competition. The state was underselling its tourism potential.

Fragmented and inefficient marketing with a shrinking budget left Georgia falling behind other southern states in visitor traffic.

The task force looked at the full spectrum of public and private tourism-related attractions and recommended actions that would enable public and private enterprises to consolidate resources and efforts in promotions and advertising.

RESULTS

- In 2005, Senate Bill 125 created the New Georgia Foundation for Tourism to coordinate marketing efforts and consolidate funding to improve the promotion of the State's tourism resources. The bill also consolidated administration of Halls of Fame to save operational and advertising costs.

- The Georgia Department of Economic Development created a long-term media and marketing plan with strong private partnership. The goal targeted a $1 billion-per-year increase in spending by tourists.

- By Executive Order, the Department of Community Affairs developed a plan for Georgia's coast, promoting sustainable future development without compromising the region's valuable and vulnerable natural environment.

COMPETITIVENESS | 2004
CHAIR: DWIGHT EVANS
CONSULTING PARTNER: ERNST & YOUNG

Despite Georgia's strong assets as a business location, the state had lost several high-profile prospects which had complained of poor communications and fragmented management in dealing with multiple economic development entities.

The task force proposed a cabinet-level workforce development office to co-ordinate development through a single executive body. They recommended focusing financial incentives on strategic industries that create high-quality jobs and incentives to draw venture capital and intellectual capital to the state.

RESULTS

- The legislature allocated a $10 million challenge grant to the Georgia Research Alliance which raised $40 million in matching contributions for a venture capital fund.

- The legislature invested $10 million in a life-sciences facilities fund.

- House Bill 389 increased tax credits for the creation of jobs paying higher-than-average salaries and offering access to health insurance.

- The Governor's Office of Workforce Development was established to spearhead a concerted effort involving employment, economic planning and education to upgrade the state's bid for higher paying jobs of the future.

TRANSPORTATION | 2007
CHAIR: NEAL PURCELL
CONSULTING PARTNER: DELOITTE

In 2004, the Administration doubled transportation spending through the Fast Forward program, expecting $15.5 billion in projects to be accomplished within six years. By year three, only 21 percent had been finished. The task force analyzed the accelerating cost – $2 billion in FY08 – of major transportation projects and the factors driving cost, construction performance and value. Task force members brought deep and wide expertise and experience in engineering, contracting and regional transportation planning.

They discovered that compared to almost all states, Georgia spent far less of its transportation budget on "new lanes" to relieve congestion – the top priority in the state system – and far more on maintenance of existing roads.

In an 85-page report, the task force detailed market forces affecting competitive bids and cost of materials, as well as government policies that may be barriers to returning the highest value on highway investments. Key interests were funding, project delivery, the design-build process and committed funds versus actual expenditures.

The task force laid out a series of measures to expedite projects and contain costs, many put in practice by the Department of Transportation.

RESULTS

- Projects that require similar contractor resources, such as cement, were spaced apart to avoid unnecessary competition or were combined for economies of scale.

- End-to-end project management significantly improved coordination. Assigning project responsibility to a single manager increased accountability and transparency.

- Value-engineering studies were required for all projects over $10 million. The contractor shared in savings as an incentive to find cost-effective options in materials and methods of construction.

- Department of Transportation representatives formed working groups with federal partners and contractors to seek ways to expedite processes and keep projects on schedule.

FREIGHT AND LOGISTICS | 2008
CHAIR: BOB FAULS
CONSULTING PARTNERS: BOOZ-ALLEN HAMILTON
CENTER OF INNOVATION FOR LOGISTICS

Freight and logistics is an economic driver in every Georgia county – so important that it's listed among the state's six Strategic Industries. One in 10 jobs in Georgia depends on shipping, storing and receiving products, generating a $300 billion economic impact. The nation's fastest growing seaport and busiest airport are Georgia-based gateways to 4,700 miles of rail and 20,000 miles of highways that carry millions of tons of freight through the state every day.

The task force conducted the first study of freight flow in Georgia and assessed the infrastructure that supports it. Their task was to map out economic opportunities linked by freight movement and how that fits into the state's larger strategic transportation plan. Recommendations focused on identifying and capitalizing on Georgia's freight and logistics assets and developing a statewide plan and business model to support industry growth.

RESULTS

- The Center of Innovation for Logistics inaugurated an annual Georgia Logistics Summit which became the largest forum for the state's industry. An annual report is published to update data used by public and private developers to identify new markets and business opportunities.

- The state's first freight and logistics plan and a comprehensive rail plan were drafted for incorporation in Georgia's strategic plan for transportation.

- A web-based Freight Mobility Exchange was created to maintain a flow of information on developments, data and resources to the industry.

- To support logistics-related education and workforce training, an inventory of state university logistics degree programs was completed as a resource for the Workforce Development Office and QuickStart training programs.

COMMERCIALIZATION/INTELLECTUAL PROPERTY | 2008
CHAIR: RICK USSERY
CONSULTING PARTNER: KAUFFMAN FOUNDATION

The State invests millions of dollars annually in university research, with the expectation that scientific breakthroughs will bring innovative companies and more high-quality jobs to Georgia.

The state's public and private universities did not have a research exchange to facilitate collaboration among scientists or provide the visibility needed to market their intellectual properties to companies shopping for development prospects. The task force recommended an enterprise-level database of patents, researchers and laboratories, designed to move more Georgia-based discoveries from lab to market.

RESULTS

- In 2009, the Georgia Research Alliance and eight public and private universities launched iResearchGeorgia, a searchable database of biomedical expertise that provides access to profiles, published papers and grant abstracts of more than 750 scientific leaders in eight public and private research universities.

- In 2010, the database had grown to nearly 9,000 grants surpassing $2.6 billion and 3,600 publications.

TASK FORCE FOCUS

WORKFORCE DEVELOPMENT | 2004
CHAIR: ANN CRAMER
CONSULTING PARTNER: IBM

"We are moving the workforce from low-wage, low-skill industries to a more knowledge-based economy and ensuring that employers can put the right people in the right jobs."

DEBRA LYONS, EXECUTIVE DIRECTOR, GOVERNOR'S OFFICE OF WORKFORCE DEVELOPMENT

In early 2004, task forces on strategic industries and competitiveness advocated aggressive action to draw high-potential, high-paying companies to business-friendly Georgia. But Georgia wasn't ready to fill the jobs in that future.

When the Workforce Development Task Force convened later that year, 40 percent of Georgia's high school students were dropping out with no diploma. At the same time, the trajectory of the job market was going higher-end in skill requirements. The market saw a 52 percent increase in openings for associate-degreed applicants. Jobs requiring technical college were projected to go up by 80 percent in the next five years.

Ann Cramer, IBM's high-energy head of corporate-community relations, chaired the task force, bringing in a team of data-driven IBM consultants.

They mapped the current workforce environment and extrapolated the findings to the logical end awaiting Georgia unless major negatives were turned around.

Their conclusions foretold a doomsday scenario: Georgia could not expect to field a workforce that was either competitive in the current market or attractive to strategic industries. Employers would exit the state or reduce their workforces here, followed by an exodus of skilled workers in search of better jobs.

"The lack of skilled workers was the key decision point for three companies to decide to locate or expand outside of Georgia," the task force report stated. It projected the consequences of resulting unemployment and deflated wages. "If left unchanged, increases in tax revenues will not cover the increased cost of social services."

On the bright side, the task force reported that Georgia had an array of high-quality programs working on various aspects of education, training and economic planning to strengthen the employment base. But the efforts were not organized to bring together the five key stakeholders in workforce planning – employers, education, government, communities and citizens – as an effective force for change.

That was the crux of the task force's recommendations. They proposed a single point of authority and accountability for developing a workforce system which aligned education, employment and economic planning. They envisioned a private non-profit corporation, led by a board comprising the Governor and the top state officials in education, labor, economic development, human services and corrections. Another pivotal recommendation was to utilize a single assessment tool statewide to identify skill gaps in the workforce in order to train resources on key needs.

The authority to create a non-profit corporation and the money to acquire state-wide technology seemed out of range – until a company marketing a proprietary assessment program pointed out certain provisions of the federal Workforce Investment Act (WIA). The WIA vests governors with the authority to appoint the state's Workforce Investment Board (WIB) and use a discretionary fund for enhancing employment programs. Georgia's WIA authority and funds had been signed over by the previous governor to the Georgia Labor Department, in contrast to Congressional intent. As a constitutional entity, the state's labor department retained exclusive use of the federal funds, amounting to about $15 million a year.

In 2006, Governor Perdue reinstated the governor's responsibility to appoint the Workforce Investment Board (WIB) and invest the funds in innovative programs. By executive order, he created the Office of Workforce Development (OWFD) to oversee the newly-constituted WIB and work with state entities and the private sector on a strategic plan to bring the task force recommendations to life.

Debra Lyons, an engineer and specialist in industrial training, was named WFD Executive Director. The timing was critical. With auto plants and military bases closing, Georgia was on the cusp of another downturn.

In August 2006, the Governor and Georgia Chamber of Commerce launched Georgia Work Ready to integrate employment and education programs with economic planning. It is the only partnership of its kind between a state government and state chamber. Much of its success has been driven by a campaign for community buy-in. This was a deliberate strategy to implement the plan at the local level state-wide, encouraging counties and regions to engage public and private partners in solving specific needs. The Work Ready spectrum reaches businesses, communities and individuals:

- Individuals earn Work Ready certification in a tier of skill levels which match job profiles developed for employers. Certified job profilers are easily reached at any of the state's technical colleges.

- Certified Work Ready Communities must meet criteria for raising their high school graduation rates and enrolling a percentage of businesses and employees in the program. More than 40 counties have met the standard, and state graduation rates are going up.

- Work Ready Regions create talent pools that target existing industries to create a network of businesses that will be a magnet for new development. Each regional effort is headed by a local business leader associated with a strategic industry.

The rapid spread of the program among communities and individuals has involved almost all of the state's 159 counties. Over 140 counties have applied for certification and are in the pipeline. Almost 120,000 Georgians earned certification in the first four years. Twenty percent score at the gold level, which qualifies for 90 percent of jobs. From March 2009 to Spring 2010, 5,000 Georgians landed a job using their Work Ready certificate. Laid-off workers can also receive gap training and incentives to offset the expense of job searches. Microsoft donated 16,000 vouchers for computer training for unemployed Georgians, available through the WFD Office.

"Georgia employers in Work Ready improve hiring success, reduce turnover, lower training costs, increase productivity and achieve higher employee morale," Lyons said. "That's impressive in any economic climate, but it's remarkable during this recession."

LANDMARKS OF BUILDING THE ECONOMY

TOURISM

SB 125 - New Georgia Foundation for Tourism – established as a public/private partnership

- Pooled funding for coordinated, aggressive marketing of state attractions
- Long-term marketing plan to increase tourism revenue $1 billion a year
- Coastal Development Plan to balance economic and environmental uses

STRATEGIC INDUSTRIES AND COMPETITIVENESS

Six strategic industries and seven supporting industries targeted for development

- Economic development teams focused on five industry areas
- Technology Enterprise Park built
- iResearch portal developed to market life-science patents for commercial development

Competitiveness initiatives increase funding and tax credits

- Legislative appropriations of $10 million seed money for $40 million match in venture capital; $10 million for life-sciences facility
- HB 389 - Tax credits for creation of higher-paying jobs
- HB 1195 -Governor's Office of Workforce Development and Work Ready program established

COMMERCIALIZING GEORGIA RESEARCH

iResearch - First single web-based source of biomedical intellectual property

- Searchable database of cross-referenced patents, grants, papers and faculty
- Participation of eight public and private research universities

TRANSPORTATION

Transportation recommendations to mitigate project cost adopted by DOT

- Spacing projects to avoid high-demand, high-price periods
- Value-engineering for all projects over $10 million
- End-to-end project manager and single manager oversight
- Working relationship with Feds to shorten timelines on projects

Freight and Logistics recognized as significant factor in economic development and transportation planning

- Center for Innovation in Logistics provides statewide data on freight flow, infrastructure, logistics-related industries
- First freight and logistics statewide plan integrated in state strategic plan for transportation

WORKFORCE DEVELOPMENT

HB 1195 – Workforce Investment Board, Office of Workforce Development, Work Ready established in law

- Unified efforts of employment, education, economic development in workforce upgrade and planning
- Work Ready certification for communities and individuals to increase competitiveness
- Individual certification to qualify unemployed applicants for available jobs

CHAPTER SEVEN

REFLECTIONS IN THE REARVIEW MIRROR: IT WAS WORTH THE RIDE

For his eight years in office, Governor Sonny Perdue held himself accountable for management performance – the government's and his own. It is a publicly undervalued but critically essential responsibility of a governing executive to ensure that the functions of the enterprise work at peak performance to deliver cost-effective value. Perdue understood that the operating system enables both the everyday activities of state and the envisioned aspirations of the future.

It's probable that too little credit will be accorded Governor Perdue's success in bringing Georgia from a mediocre performance evaluation to the top tier of "best-managed states." There are no monuments on Capitol grounds for that kind of achievement.

But many of Georgia's most respected citizens have been witnesses to the quiet revolution and gave their efforts to the cause – corporate executives of high repute, hundreds of accomplished professionals among the state's citizenry, dozens of internationally respected consultants, and public servants throughout government.

This chapter gives voice to their recognition and participation.

"We never put on the label 'blue-ribbon commission'. We were a private-sector Special Ops unit... targeting operations where smart business strategies could help government work better and cost less. We covered a lot of territory in seven years, and most of the change was under the radar."

BOB HATCHER, CEO, MIDCOUNTRY FINANCIAL

CO-CHAIR, COMMISSION FOR A NEW GEORGIA

It's natural to want to wax wistful looking back at seven years of steadfast effort, awed by how much was accomplished. But sentimentality would not be in character with the Commission's workmanlike focus on action and results, always going forward.

The Commission for A New Georgia went about its public-sector work in the businesslike way that its private-sector leaders conducted their enterprises. They expected a regular report to shareholders to show results, which in this case were inside-government factors that impacted the public interest.

The reason the Commission stayed together as a team and on the job for seven years was found in those shareholder reports. They were delivered and discussed at every quarterly meeting to bring news of action, progress and outcomes of CNG-recommended reforms. At the same time, new task forces were moving into the next projects as the flywheel went round.

The cycle of productivity was continuous. It birthed many firsts for state government, some which prior commissions had tried for decades to bring to term.

The Commission's way was not to seek the spotlight, nor to shun it if a beam turned their way. Press attention was occasional and minimal, but for those who had the interest to read about a business-led initiative to make government work better, there was considerable ink spread in publications like *Georgia Trend, Georgia Contractor, Governing* and *Reason*. A 2008 article in The Pew Charitable Trust's nationally read *Trust Magazine* signaled that business-as-usual was indeed changing in Georgia:

> Georgia, under Perdue, has been one of the leaders in the push to make governments run better by importing and adapting management techniques, information systems and performance measures from the business world.

For the public record, the Commission provided a website as a repository for all task force reports, CNG business, information updates and a running scorecard of results. The Commission's advocacy of transparency and accountability in government applied just as much to their public business.

THE GOAL TO BE THE NATION'S BEST-MANAGED STATE – which at first seemed a less-than-ringing call to "Charge!" – stuck as a title to be sought and won. On March 8, 2008, everyone in the Governor's Office and agency headquarters awaited the news. It was the day the Pew Center on the States and *Governing* magazine posted the grades for the triennial report card. The letdown was palpable: Georgia didn't make the expected A. The consolation was that no state did. The highest grade earned by three states was A-minus, and Georgia was just a tick short, one of five states with a B-plus. But it was a giant leap for Georgia from the ranks of mediocrity to the top tier. Georgia was the highest-rated state in the Southeast, and by total score was one of the top five states in the nation.

Susan Urahn, director of the Pew Center on the States, pronounced Georgia the most improved state in the 2008 evaluation. Governor Perdue was in Washington, D.C. for the announcement, one of the two governors invited to talk about managing for value and performance. *Governing's* profile of Georgia's evaluation opened this way:

> In 2003, when Governor Sonny Perdue decided to set up his Commission for A New Georgia, it sounded like a recipe for one more unread

manifesto doomed to gather more dust than interest…but the Governor meant business. And since its creation the commission has been slowly, quietly and deliberately infiltrating Georgia state government with best practices from private industry.

The ultimate claim to the best-managed title may be destined to elude Georgia and its 49 rivals. Starting with the 2011 review, Pew's Government Performance Project (GPP) changed its evaluation process. Under the new plan, management areas will be individually evaluated, one a year, on a four-year rotation. That means no more comprehensive report card to claim a spot in national rankings. The GPP's value to states is not diminished in terms of the performance assessment and prescription for improvement. This worked to Georgia's advantage in many ways. Implementation Director Jeff Strane called the GPP "our scorecard."

"It's the best one out there. It represents what we thought to be the fairest approach to measuring the management of government," Strane said.

But, alas, the touted Best-Managed State winner's cup will be nobody's trophy.

The Governor, Jim Lientz, Tommy Hills and anyone else who led the charge will say that the best-managed slogan served its purpose, but the real value was always about testing Georgia's performance by an external evaluator and benchmarking against other states as well as Georgia's own progress points. Georgia was tested – and scored in the 90th percentile. In many grade books, that's an A.

The all-important goal was met. Reform and improvement swept through every management area of government. That is the legacy of the Perdue Administration and the Commission for A New Georgia.

THE SCRIPTURE ABOUT PROPHETS BEING NOT WITHOUT HONOR except in their own land could be a fair statement about the Commission for A New Georgia. While its own state was mostly oblivious to CNG's work, the nation began to pay attention.

The National Governors Association bestowed its two top awards for distinguished service by a private citizen and by a public servant to leaders of the Commission and the Office of Implementation. In 2006, Lonice Barrett won NGA's most prestigious service award, which was presented by the association's then-chair Governor Mike Huckabee. In 2010, Commission co-chairs Joe Rogers and Bob Hatcher were jointly honored with the highest award for contributions by a private citizen to state government, presented at the annual meeting in Boston.

Governor Sonny Perdue was named a 2009 Innovator of the Year by the Reason Foundation for his vision and development of a business model for state government operations. "Amidst today's massive deficits and red ink, we need government leaders who are willing to ditch the failed status quo and seek out better ways of doing things," said Reason's director of governmental reform Leonard Gilroy. He saw the Commission as an example for other states:

> "Smart public managers recognize that while you may not be able to run government like a business, you can and should integrate best practices from the business sector whenever possible to stay nimble, efficient and responsive. The Commission for A New Georgia has been a pioneer and a proven leader in bringing private-sector thinking and innovation to bear on state services. It has focused on action and results, delivering tens of millions in savings to the state and improving services for Georgia taxpayers. Leaders in every state would be smart to learn from and replicate the CNG model."

Perdue was tapped as one of eight governors selected to serve as charter members of the Pew Center's Future States Council. *Governing* chose Georgia to host its annual Managing Performance conference, with Perdue as keynote speaker. *Governing's* publisher said the selection was influenced by the Governor's "sustained commitment to improving government management and enhancing public service."

The Council on State Governments has recognized both the Commission's work and the Customer Service initiative as finalists for innovation awards. In 2010, the Boston-based Pioneer Institute named the Commission for A New Georgia a winner in the nationwide Better Government competition.

Individual awards for innovation were presented to projects that developed from Commission recommendations. Two examples: The State Properties Commission's web-based Building, Lands and Leases Inventory of Property won the national innovation award from the National Association of State Facility Administrators. And the State Purchasing Department's work on a spend analytics model was chosen as one of three "lab states" projects funded by the Pew Center as a national prototype for tracking purchasing expenditures.

Bragging is the not the Commission's style. But it's nice to be recognized.

As AMERICA DEALS WITH THE CRASHING CONSEQUENCES of business and government management failures, states are paying greater attention to how well officials in their bureaucracies are minding the store. They're looking for models of successful management reform that work swiftly and surely to change business-as-usual. That would describe the Commission for A New Georgia, and other states have been asking for the instruction manual.

More important for Georgia has been the recognition by other state leadership that management matters. In 2010, a special Senate budget committee, formed by Lieutenant Governor Casey Cagle, reported 50 recommendations for long-term solutions for sustainable budgets. Task force members included private-sector business leaders and public policy thinkers. More than half of the solutions echo or expand on Commission recommendations which have been implemented. The embracing of the best-managed state goal by the legislature and future administrations was the ultimate hoped-for outcome and best testament to the value of the Commission for A New Georgia's seven years in government.

The *Atlanta Journal-Constitution* ran a full-page Editorial Board Opinion after the drastically-cut 2009 budget was signed. It asked many of the same questions that CNG task forces had addressed about managing a sustainable government, and it recognized the Commission approach as a way to answers:

> Governor Sonny Perdue convened the Commission for A New Georgia to draft a blueprint for moving us into the ranks of the best-managed states. Notable progress has been made toward that worthy goal, but state leaders, business interests and other vested parties need to do more. The commission might be a good model of how to approach this challenge. We'd like for Georgia to be the best-led state coming out of this painful recession. Achieving that will require sound leadership and creativity

that takes risks and pushes outside political boxes. A good place to start would be taking a blue-sky look at state government with an eye toward seeking efficiencies beyond what Governor Perdue's process work has already gained.

The high stakes of managing for value does not enhance the discipline's glitter as a high-profile star of campaign politics. It's the wonk-work described by *Atlanta Journal-Constitution* columnist Jim Wooten, who was getting the picture ahead of his colleagues:

> Perdue's efforts are modernizing the state's day-to-day business affairs, the humdrum stuff that has no political benefit whatsoever but is absolutely vital. The state has long needed somebody to tend to the dull stuff: counting the cars, locating property, consolidating the leases, managing properties to lower costs, planning for the transition of a state work force that will lose to retirement 25 percent of its experienced employees over the next five years. If it's done really well, nobody notices.

THE LAST WORD BELONGS TO THOSE WHO SERVED

THE GOOD WORDS OF OTHERS are gratifying and validating to all who have made the work of the Commission their business for seven years.

But the true judges of the value of the mission and the effort that went into it are those private citizens who accepted the responsibility for making a difference in their government and who undertook the venture and saw it through to success. The members of the Commission for A New Georgia have the final say – in their own words – about the worthiness of the endeavor and its achievements.

They speak to common themes: Governor Perdue's accountability for leadership and results; the absence of politics in the mission; the recognition of what business can bring to better government; and appreciation for the opportunity to make a contribution to their state.

Their voice speaks to the hundreds of Georgians who gave their time and talent to make Georgia one of the nation's best-managed states.

Listen, all Georgians, with pride.

"We do not often see elected officials reach out to solicit best-practice input from the private sector. Governor Perdue personally drove the implementation of significant private-sector input on how to improve government efficiency. The process has created a real win-win collaboration that should be a model for the future of this state and for that matter, the nation."

DAVID RATCLIFFE, PRESIDENT AND CEO, THE SOUTHERN COMPANY

"There is great knowledge in this business community. Some of these best minds are anxious and happy to apply their skills to the issues of our state and society. Working with the Commission gave me much greater perspective on opportunities and limitations at the state level – a deeper appreciation for the challenges the State has to deal with in reality. The Commission has set a pattern of public/private partnership that can be emulated in future administrations."

ARTHUR BLANK, CHAIRMAN, ARTHUR M. BLANK FAMILY FOUNDATION
CO-FOUNDER OF THE HOME DEPOT
OWNER OF ATLANTA FALCONS

"It quickly became clear that the Governor was very serious about this. He has been to every meeting, doesn't delegate the leadership and has been actively interested in getting a better solution. Most of the people on this Commission have been invited to join other activities where the initial idea is great, but there is no follow-through. In this case, there was a ton of follow-through. There were good people who were asked to lead the Commission's efforts. It's been a worthwhile effort for everyone who has been a part of it."

JOHN RICE, VICE CHAIRMAN OF GENERAL ELECTRIC
PRESIDENT AND CHIEF EXECUTIVE OFFICER OF GE INFRASTRUCTURE

"The Governor's approach to take politics out of progress initiatives and change has enabled our business community in Georgia to contribute significant ideas – which have been implemented. The Commission's positive impact on state government has resulted in innovation and dramatically improved customer service."

RICHARD ANTHONY, CHAIRMAN OF THE BOARD AND CEO, SYNOVUS

"The Commission for A New Georgia has permitted people with legacies of accomplishment to come together not only to discuss problems but to create blueprints for the solution of many of the state's challenges. Unlike many paper plans and studies, it has allowed those same people to participate in and monitor the solutions…the impacts on state government have been nothing short of profound.

ERROLL DAVIS, CHANCELLOR, UNIVERSITY SYSTEM OF GEORGIA

"Future administrations should most definitely expand the mission of the Commission for A New Georgia in order to bring to state government the best the private sector has to offer and find legitimate fits for the collective thinking of a group of the State's best minds from business, philanthropy, academia and public service."

EARL LEONARD, SENIOR VICE PRESIDENT (RET.), THE COCA-COLA COMPANY

"'Smart' and 'government' are not two words usually linked, but I am encouraged at the progress being made. The Commission meetings start before sunrise at the Governor's mansion. Invariably, as I fight through the traffic to get there, I wonder—'Is this really a good way to spend my pre-dawn hours?' Then I hear the reports, feel the excitement and see the advancements. Our work is mostly behind the scenes, but the goal is clear. 'Good enough for government work' just isn't good enough anymore."

DINK NESMITH, CHAIRMAN, COMMUNITY NEWSPAPERS, INC.

"Government, to be effective, should be simple, direct, efficient, and workable. This is what the Commission for A New Georgia was about, and through the efforts of many dedicated people, including Governor Perdue, I believe the Commission achieved these goals. I am proud I was a member."

LARRY WALKER, ATTORNEY AT LAW
FORMER MAJORITY LEADER OF THE GEORGIA HOUSE OF REPRESENTATIVES

"The Commission for A New Georgia demonstrated the benefit of using private sector business expertise to improve how state government delivers services to the public. Answering the question, 'How can we do this better and more cost efficiently?' became the driver for numerous CNG task forces resulting in better service for the public and millions of dollars in cost savings. Governor Perdue's leadership and commitment to implement recommendations from the CNG made the whole process work."

BRUCE COOK, FOUNDER AND CEO, CHOOSING THE BEST

"There are many areas in state government that are now operating more efficiently as a result of the recommendations made by the Commission for A New Georgia. It has been an honor to serve with the commission and be involved in the good work it has done."

J. ROY ROWLAND, M.D., RETIRED CONGRESSMAN

"The Commission became an important catalyst for saying that new thoughts, ideas and ways of doing business are open. And with that the Governor was saying, 'This is what the New Georgia is all about.' CNG provided concrete, reliable, trustworthy information that was used to shape and deliver the services of the government."

CARL SWEARINGEN, PERDUE TRANSITION CHAIR
EXECUTIVE CONSULTANT OF THE KALEIDESCOPE GROUP

NATIONAL GOVERNOR'S ASSOCIATION HONORS CNG FOR DISTINGUISHED SERVICE

Lonice Barrett (*left*) with Arkansas Governor Mike Huckabee.

Commssion Co-chair Bob Hatcher (*left*) with Vermont Governor Jim Douglas.

In 2006 and 2010, the National Governor's Association bestowed its highest awards for Distinguished Service to leaders representing Georgia's public-private partnership in the Commission for A New Georgia and Governor's Office of Implementation.

In 2006, Lonice Barrett was honored with NGA's top award for public service to a state, presented by NGA Chairman Mike Huckabee, Governor of Arkansas.

In 2010, Commission Co-chairs Bob Hatcher and Joe Rogers shared the NGA's most prestigious award for service to state government by a private citizen. Hatcher attended the NGA Annual Conference in Boston and accepted the award on behalf of the Commission from NGA Chair Jim Douglas, Governor of Vermont.

APPENDICES

GOVERNOR SONNY PERDUE: *"PUT ME IN, COACH!"*

Sonny Perdue didn't grow up daydreaming about a future as Governor of Georgia. The Gold Dome was a world away from the family farm in Middle Georgia, where his father raised produce and his mother taught school. But the lessons of tilling and planting and harvesting were always with him, cultivating his values and the principles he applied wherever his life's work led.

> "Growing up on a farm teaches you to do things in order. You can't harvest before you plant. You can't plant before you prepare the ground. There was an order and timing in the progression of growth and ultimately the benefits it produced. I watched and learned, from about eight years old, the role of purposeful, meaningful work and accomplishment, and I found fulfillment in it."

The farm boy eventually did get to the big city, trucking produce to the Atlanta market as soon as he got his driver's license. At age 16, Sonny Perdue's apprenticeship in the business side of the agri-enterprise had begun. "I was handling big rolls of cash, sleeping out on a cot at the farmers' market. That gave me an appreciation of cash management," Governor Perdue remembers.

By the time he started high school, he was already motivated by a work ethic that focused on achievement, and it translated well in both academics and athletics. It also drove a new ambition to go into a business that offered more financial security than the fluctuating farm economy.

Playing sports taught Perdue life lessons as well – he would never be satisfied sitting on the sidelines if he could get in the game. With that vigor, he played baseball for Warner Robins High school and quarterbacked the Demons in football. "Both of those are high-touch experiences in athletics. So all my life it was, 'Put me in, Coach,'" said the Governor.

His plan was to graduate from the University of Georgia with a doctorate of veterinary medicine, a rigorous science discipline which required the highest grades for acceptance. And he intended to play football for the Bulldogs while he was there. He did them both.

He served in the Air Force after college, rising to captain and gaining hands-on experience in operations and leadership in a government organization. After a brief career as a practicing vet, he went on to own and operate successful agribusinesses with locations across the Southeast.

By then, he and his wife Mary were raising an active family in Houston County, and he was serving in civic affairs. While he was in his tenth year on the local planning board, the state senator in his district decided to retire from public service. More than once, Sonny Perdue was pressed to put his name on the ballot, and more than once, he declined. A trip to Williamsburg with Mary changed his mind, and once again, he chose to get in the game instead of cheering from the stands.

"I actually got caught up in the spirit of the founding fathers and their commitment to citizen service. We have a citizen legislature with two-year terms. Mary and I thought and prayed about it and concluded we could survive anything for two years," he says, laughing.

Senator Perdue went into office with Governor Zell Miller and Lieutenant Governor Pierre Howard and began his 11-year legislative career. By the end of his first session, he was chafing at the bit to push harder on the productivity and progress of legislative action.

"I had the determination that if I was going to be in the legislature, I wanted to be engaged and part of the process," Governor Perdue said. "I remember writing Pierre Howard a personal letter after my first session because I had become anxious about the slow progress of things. I told him that I had left my business, my family, all of my obligations back home to serve, so 'Put me in, Coach.'"

The Lieutenant Governor took the freshman Senator up on the offer, assigning him responsibilities to demonstrate his ability to work hard, attend to detail and get things done. Senator Perdue became Majority Leader after four years and President Pro Tempore after six years.

Even as a senate leader, he was frustrated by the "buddy system" that ruled the chamber. During his terms, he earned a reputation for courage in tackling tough issues and for his grasp of complex problems. He was recognized as a leading authority on agriculture, transportation, education, energy, emerging technologies and economic development.

In 2001, he left the Senate to run for Governor as a Republican on a platform of restoring public trust in state government and eliminating bureaucratic interference in people's lives. His candidacy was a long-shot against an incumbent Democrat in a state that hadn't elected a Republican governor in 127 years. Candidate Perdue wasn't daunted by the odds.

"It goes back to the focused, determined little farm boy who goes out there and says 'I'm gonna do this, and I'm gonna give it all I can,'" he said. "The thing about Mary and me is that once we decided to run, we would have felt just as victorious, win or lose, because we did what we were called to do and fulfilled our commitment to ourselves, our faith and the people we were advocating for."

He stunned political observers by taking down a seemingly invincible sitting governor, and on January 13, 2003, Sonny Perdue was sworn in as Georgia's 81st Governor. He was re-elected in 2006 with 56 percent of the vote in a year many Republicans nationwide lost their seats.

Governor Perdue immediately brought new perspective to governing, moving towards a managerial style of performance-based decisions.

"I knew that Georgia needed to move into modern-day governing, which I equate with value," he said. "When I took office, I became a facts-based decision-maker. I had been in business in a competitive agriculture industry where I needed to be customer-focused, data-driven and results-oriented. Those were the principles I brought with me to make decisions I thought would give the best value."

He has dedicated his administration to transforming Georgia's government to a 21st Century enterprise, attracting new businesses and jobs to Georgia and improving the quality of programs that touch the lives of children.

Governor Perdue's "Put me in, Coach," attitude has led to results on the scoreboard. His tenure has been highlighted by success in raising high school graduation rates, focusing on economic development in both urban and rural areas of the state, and re-engineering the workings of government to deliver better value for citizens.

And under the leadership of Governor Sonny Perdue, Georgia has gone from middle-of-the-road rankings to earning recognition as one of the top five Best-Managed State in America.

APPENDIX B

COMMISSION FOR A NEW GEORGIA: OFFICERS AND MEMBERS

CHAIRS

ROBERT HATCHER
President and CEO, MidCountry Financial Corporation

JOE W. ROGERS, JR.
Chairman, President and CEO, Waffle House, Inc.

MEMBERS

DAN AMOS
Chairman and CEO, Aflac, Inc.

RICHARD ANTHONY
Chairman and CEO, Synovus

ARTHUR M. BLANK
Chairman, Arthur M. Blank Family Foundation

ROBERT L. BROWN
President and CEO, Robert L. Brown Associates, Inc.

ANNA CABLIK
President, Anatek, Inc., President and CEO of Anasteel & Supply Company

JOHN CAY
Chairman, Wachovia Insurance Services

BRUCE COOK
CEO and President, Choosing the Best

ERROLL DAVIS
Chancellor, University System of Georgia

KIRBY GODSEY
Chancellor, Mercer University

RUSTY GRIFFIN
President, Griffin LLC

BILL JONES III
Chairman of the Board and CEO, Sea Island Co.

FRANK JONES
Partner, King and Spalding (Retired)

EARL T. LEONARD, JR.
Senior Vice President for Corporate Affairs, The Coca Cola Company (Retired)

DINK NESMITH
President, Community Newspapers, Inc.

NEAL PURCELL
Partner, KPMG (Retired)

DAVID RATCLIFFE
Chairman, President and CEO, Southern Company

ROBERT RATLIFF
CEO and Chairman of the Board, AGCO, Inc.

JOHN RICE
Vice Chairman, General Electric and President and CEO, General Electric Technology Infrastructure

ROY ROWLAND, M.D.
Former U.S. Congressman, 8th District of Georgia

DAVID SATCHER M.D.
Director, Satcher Health Leadership Institute, Morehouse School of Medicine

BETTY SIEGEL
President Emeritus, Kennesaw State University

CARL SWEARINGEN
Executive Consultant, The Kaleidescope Group

RICK USSERY
Chairman of the Board and Chief Executive Officer of TSYS (Retired)

LARRY WALKER
Attorney at Law, Walker, Hulbert, Gray & Byrd

PHILLIP WILHEIT
President, Wilheit Packaging

COMMISSION FOR A NEW GEORGIA BOARD MEMBERS

Leaders of great success, lives of great service

COMMISSION CO-CHAIRS

ROBERT HATCHER
PRESIDENT AND CEO, MIDCOUNTRY FINANCIAL CORP.

Mr. Hatcher has served as Chairman of the University System of Georgia Board of Regents and chairman of the Georgia Chamber of Commerce. He is a graduate of the University of Georgia and the School of Banking of the South.

JOE W. ROGERS, JR.
CHAIRMAN, PRESIDENT AND CEO, WAFFLE HOUSE, INC.

Mr. Rogers has served as a trustee of the Georgia Tech Foundation, the Woodruff Arts Center, the ESR Children's Health Care System, the Atlanta History Center and the Atlanta Chamber of Commerce. He is a graduate of the Georgia Institute of Technology and Harvard University.

COMMISSION MEMBERS

DAN AMOS
CHAIRMAN AND CEO, AFLAC, INC.

Mr. Amos launched the Aflac Duck to advertising fame. He chaired the University of Georgia Foundation and has served as a director of the Synovus Financial Corporation. Additionally, Mr. Amos has been a trustee of Children's Healthcare of Atlanta and the House of Mercy. He is a graduate of the University of Georgia.

RICHARD ANTHONY
CHAIRMAN AND CEO, SYNOVUS

Mr. Anthony has served as director of the American Bankers Association. He has been a leader of the Georgia Chamber of Commerce as well as in the State of Georgia Economic Development Commission. He is a graduate of the University of Alabama and the University of Virginia.

ARTHUR M. BLANK
CHAIRMAN, ARTHUR M. BLANK FAMILY FOUNDATION
OWNER, ATLANTA FALCONS

Mr. Blank, co-founder of the Home Depot, serves as Chairman, President and CEO of AMB Group, LLC. He is the owner and CEO of the Atlanta Falcons and the Georgia Force. Mr. Blank has served as a trustee of the Carter Center, Emory University and the Cooper Institute. He is a graduate of Babson College.

ROBERT L. BROWN
PRESIDENT AND CEO, ROBERT L. BROWN ASSOCIATES INC.

Mr. Brown, Fellow of the American Institute of Architects, chaired the Georgia Partnership of Excellence in Education. He has served on the foundations of Southern Polytechnic State University and Georgia Perimeter College and as a trustee of Agnes Scott College. Mr. Brown has served on the State Transportation Board and the corporate boards of Georgia Power and the Georgia Chamber of Commerce.

ANNA CABLIK
PRESIDENT, ANATEK, INC.
PRESIDENT AND CEO OF ANASTEEL & SUPPLY CO.

Ms. Cablik has served as a director of the Georgia Power Company and on the boards of Branch Banking & Trust, the Greater Atlanta Economic Alliance and Microenterprise Strategy at United Way of Metropolitan Atlanta.

JOHN CAY
CHAIRMAN, WACHOVIA INSURANCE SERVICES

Mr. Cay was chairman of the nation's ninth largest insurance brokerage and employee benefits consulting firm. He has served as president of the trustees of the Telfair Museum. He is a graduate of the University of North Carolina at Chapel Hill and attended the management program at the Harvard Business School.

BRUCE COOK
CEO AND PRESIDENT, CHOOSING THE BEST

Mr. Cook has chaired the Board of the Department of Human Resources. He serves on the board of the Department of Community Health and as board chair for the National Abstinence Education Association (NAEA). He is a graduate of The Georgia Institute of Technology and the Harvard University Graduate School of Business.

ERROLL DAVIS
CHANCELLOR, UNIVERSITY SYSTEM OF GEORGIA

Mr. Davis was CEO, president and board chair of Alliant Energy Corporation. He chaired the Carnegie Mellon board of trustees, served as a trustee of the University of Chicago and has been a member of the University of Wisconsin Board of Regents, Southern Regional Education Board and the National Commission on Energy Policy. He is a graduate of Carnegie Mellon and the University of Chicago.

KIRBY GODSEY, PH.D.
CHANCELLOR, MERCER UNIVERSITY

Dr. Godsey has served on the Executive Council of the College Commission for the Southern Association of Colleges and Schools and the Executive Committee of the National Association of Independent Colleges and Universities. He holds degrees from Samford University, New Orleans Baptist Theological Seminary, the University of Alabama and Tulane University.

RUSTY GRIFFIN
PRESIDENT, GRIFFIN LLC

Mr. Griffin has served as director of the Georgia Chamber of Commerce and is a member of the Georgia Council on Economic Education, the Georgia Partnership for Excellence in Education, and the Chemical Producers and Distributors Association. He is a trustee of the University of Georgia Foundation.

BILL JONES III
CHAIRMAN OF THE BOARD AND CEO, SEA ISLAND CO.

Mr. Jones has served as trustee and chairman of the Georgia Research Alliance and Georgia Cancer Coalition and chaired the Georgia Ports Authority. He has been director of the Georgia Chamber of Commerce and chaired the Georgia Historical Society Board of Curators. Mr. Jones is a graduate of Valdosta State University.

FRANK JONES
PARTNER, KING AND SPALDING (RETIRED)

Mr. Jones has served as Of Counsel to Jones, Cork & Miller LLP. He has also served as trustee of Emory University, Wesleyan College and as a director of The Carter Center.

EARL T. LEONARD, JR.
SENIOR VICE PRESIDENT FOR CORPORATE AFFAIRS, THE COCA COLA COMPANY. (RETIRED)

Mr. Leonard has served as Executive-in-Residence for the University of Georgia Terry College of Business, as a trustee of the University of Georgia Foundation and of the Richard B. Russell Foundation, and as president of the University of Georgia Alumni Society.

DINK NESMITH
PRESIDENT, COMMUNITY NEWSPAPERS, INC.

Mr. Nesmith has served on the University System of Georgia Board of Regents and chaired the Fanning Institute for Leadership. He has served as director of Athens First Bank and Trust, Southern Mutual Insurance Company and Pattillo Construction Company. Mr. Nesmith is a graduate of the University of Georgia.

NEAL PURCELL
PARTNER, KPMG (RETIRED)

Mr. Purcell retired from the KPMG board of directors, having served as managing partner for the Northwest and the Southeast regions and vice chairman of operations for the firm's national audit practice. He has served on the boards of the Southern Company, Synovus Financial Corporation and Kaiser Permanente.

DAVID RATCLIFFE
CHAIRMAN, PRESIDENT AND CEO, SOUTHERN COMPANY

Mr. Ratcliffe has chaired the Edison Electric Institute, the Georgia Research Alliance and the Georgia Chamber of Commerce. He has served as a director of the Federal Reserve Bank of Atlanta and CSX Transportation. Mr. Ratcliffe has been a trustee of the Woodruff Arts Center and a member of the Georgia Partnership for Excellence in Education. He is a graduate of Valdosta State University and the Woodrow Wilson College of Law.

ROBERT RATLIFF
CEO AND CHAIRMAN OF THE BOARD, AGCO, INC.

Mr. Ratliff has chaired The Manufacturing Institute and served on the Board of Councilors of The Carter Center and as a director of Kysor Industry Corporation and the Equipment Manufacturers Institute. He is a graduate of the University of Maryland and the M.I.T. Sloan School Senior Executive Program.

JOHN RICE
VICE CHAIRMAN, GE
PRESIDENT AND CEO, GE TECHNOLOGY INFRASTRUCTURE

Mr. Rice has served as a trustee of Emory University, the Walker School, and Hamilton College. He was chair of the Metro Atlanta Chamber of Commerce and a member of the International Advisory Board of King Fahd University in Saudi Arabia. He is a graduate of Hamilton College.

ROY ROWLAND, M.D.
FORMER U.S. CONGRESSMAN, 8ᵀᴴ DISTRICT OF GEORGIA

Dr. Rowland served in Congress from 1983-1995 and in the Georgia House of Representatives from 1976-1982. He is a graduate of the Medical College of Georgia and is a World War II Army veteran.

DAVID SATCHER, M.D., PH.D.
DIRECTOR, SATCHER HEALTH LEADERSHIP INSTITUTE, MOREHOUSE SCHOOL OF MEDICINE

Dr. Satcher served as the 16th Surgeon General of the United States and interim president of Morehouse School of Medicine. He has been a fellow of the Kaiser Family Foundation, the American Academy of Family Physicians, the American College of Preventive Medicine and the American College of Physicians. He is a graduate of Morehouse College and Case Western Reserve University.

BETTY SIEGEL, PH.D.
PRESIDENT EMERITUS, KENNESAW STATE UNIVERSITY

Dr. Siegel is the former president of Kennesaw State University where she holds the Distinguished Chair of Leadership, Ethics & Character. She has served on the Board of Directors for the Character Education Partnership, and was co-founder of the International Alliance for Invitational Education. She has degrees from Wake Forest University, the University of North Carolina at Chapel Hill, Florida State University and Indiana University.

CARL SWEARINGEN
EXECUTIVE CONSULTANT, THE KALEIDESCOPE GROUP

Mr. Swearingen retired as senior vice president and corporate secretary of the BellSouth Corporation. He chaired the boards of the Technical Colleges System and Department of Industry, Trade and Tourism and served on the boards of the Georgia Chamber of Commerce, Atlanta Chamber of Commerce, University of Georgia Foundation, and Berry College. He is a graduate of the University of Georgia and the Massachusetts Institute of Technology.

RICK USSERY
CHAIRMAN OF THE BOARD AND CHIEF EXECUTIVE OFFICER OF TSYS
(RETIRED)

Mr. Ussery has served as a director of Georgia Power Company and on the Columbus State University Foundation board. He graduated from Auburn University, Duke University's Fuqua School of Executive Management and Rutgers University's Stonier School of Banking.

LARRY WALKER
ATTORNEY AT LAW, WALKER, HULBERT, GRAY & BYRD

Mr. Walker served in the Georgia House of Representatives from 1986-2002 as Administration Floor Leader and as Majority Leader. He has sat on the board of the Georgia Department of Transportation, and on the Board of Regents of the University System of Georgia and was an International Business Fellow. Mr. Walker graduated from the University of Georgia Law School.

PHILLIP WILHEIT
PRESIDENT, WILHEIT PACKAGING

Mr. Wilheit has chaired the Georgia Chamber of Commerce and Gainesville/Hall Development Authority. He serves on the Georgia Department of Economic Development. He chaired the board of Gainesville Bank and Trust as well as GB&T Bancshares.

APPENDIX C

COMMISSION FOR A NEW GEORGIA: TASK FORCE CHAIRS AND MEMBERS

Bringing the best thinking and best practices
to the making of a Best-Managed State

SPACE MANAGEMENT | 2004

CHAIR: LARRY GELLERSTEDT
President and CEO,
Cousins Properties Inc.
Atlanta

CLAY BOARDMAN
President, Enterprise Mill, LLC
Augusta

LISA BORDERS
Senior Vice President, Cousins Properties
Atlanta

ED BOWEN
Principal, Real Estate Strategies
Atlanta

ANN CRAMER
Director, Corporate Community
Relations, IBM Corporation
Atlanta

HAROLD DAWSON JR.
President, Harold A. Dawson Company
Atlanta

DANA GAVIN
Geico Insurance
Lake Park

MICKEY MCGUIRE
Office of Planning & Budget
Atlanta

JOSH MOORE
Attorney, The Southern Company
Norcross

FRANK NORTON JR.
President, The Norton Agency
Gainesville

DON PERRY
President, LaVista Associates
Norcross

NANCY QUAN SELLERS
Vice President, Ackerman & Company
Atlanta

TRED SHURLING
The Shurling Company
Macon

ASHLEY VAN BUREN
ALLYSON WATKINS
The Gellerstedt Group
Atlanta

CONSULTANTS: IBM

RICHARD HARRISON
GEORGE JARVIS
DIANA SWEETWOOD
JOHN WILSON

OFFICE OF PLANNING & BUDGET

ROBERT GIACOMINI

CAPITAL CONSTRUCTION | 2004

CHAIR: JIM CARSON,
Chief Executive Officer,
Carter & Associates (Retired)
Atlanta

CLARA AXAM
Enterprise Foundation
Atlanta

HAK-KEUN CHANG
U.S. Department of Housing & Urban Development
Dunwoody

JUDY GRAMMER
Grammer Construction
Rock Spring

OSCAR HARRIS
Turner & Associates
Atlanta

SAM HOLMES
C.B. Richard Ellis
Atlanta

JIMMY LANIER
Lanier, Brookins
Statesboro

RON NAWROCKI
Office of Planning & Budget
Atlanta

ENNIS PARKER
The Facility Group
Smyrna

JIM PHILIPS
Hatfield, Phillips
Decatur

TOMMY RAGSDALE
Thomas Ragsdale & Associates
Albany

ROY RANKIN
Rankin & Associates
Tifton

DARRELL ROCHESTER
Rochester & Associates
Gainesville

SUSAN THOMAS
Susan S. Thomas, Architect
Rome

SCOTT THOMPSON
Piedmont Construction
Macon

AL TRUJILLO
Recall Corporation
Norcross

CONSULTANTS: ACCENTURE
REGINALD EWING
CATHARINE KELLY
BOB MCCULLOCH

OFFICE OF PLANNING & BUDGET
ROBERT GIACOMINI

TOURISM | 2004

CHAIR: PHIL JACOBS
Retired President,
AT&T (formerly BellSouth)
Atlanta

HAROLD BEVIS
Delta Airlines
Atlanta

STEPHANIE BLANK
The Arthur M. Blank Family Foundation
Atlanta

JEFF HAIDET
MeKenna, Long and Aldridge
Atlanta

HOPPY HOPKINS
Reddick Construction Co.
Thomaston

KAREN KIMBREL
The Colquitt/Miller Arts Council
Colquitt

JESUS LOPEZ
South America Fiesta
Marietta

JON MANNS
Dekalb Convention & Visitors Bureau
Decatur

SHARAD PATEL
Windsor Hotel
Americus

BRENDA PRICE
Georgia Association of Convention and
Visitor Bureaus
Columbus

MARK SMITH
Mulberry Inn
Savannah

TAMMY STOUT
Augusta Sports Council
Augusta

GENE WEEKS
Six Flags Theme Park
Marietta

ALTON WINGATE
Community Bankshares, Inc.
Cornelia

BILL JONES
Sea Island Company
Sea Island

**CONSULTANTS: GEORGIA TECH
ECONOMIC DEVELOPMENT**
ANN O'NEILL
TERRY GANDY
MITCHELL KENYATTA

LEADERSHIP DEVELOPMENT | 2004

CHAIR: LEE LEE JAMES
Vice Chairman and Chief People Officer,
Synovus Financial Corp.
Columbus

DAVID BOYD
Director, Deloitte
Pittsburgh

NEDRA FARRAR-LUTEN
Hartsfield International Airport
Atlanta

BOB FLIGHT
Sea Island Company
Sea Island

JERRY FULKS
West Georgia Healthcare
LaGrange

JUDGE GREG GRAYSON
Catoosa County Probate Court
Ringgold

DINORAH HALL
James H. Hall Eye Center
Albany

ANGIE HART
AFLAC
Columbus

ED HESS
Goizueta Business School,
Emory University
Atlanta

DR. DAVID MILLS
J.W. Fanning Institute,
University of Georgia
Athens

PAT PITTARD
Heidrick & Struggles
Atlanta

DR. MARY SUE POLLEYS
Columbus State University
Columbus

MARTHA REABOLD
Habersham Bank
Cornelia

DEACON JOE RUBERTE
Holy Spirit Catholic Center
Atlanta

DON SPEAKS
Don Speaks and Associates
Stone Mountain

SARALYN STAFFORD
Georgia Academy for Economic
Development
Douglas

BERNARD TAYLOR
Alston & Bird LLP
Atlanta

ANGELICA WOLF
Acceptance Insurance
Dalton

**CONSULTANT: CARL VINSON
INSTITUTE, UNIVERSITY OF
GEORGIA**
WES WYNENS

ADMINISTRATIVE SERVICES | 2004

CHAIR: JIM COPELAND
CEO, Deloitte & Touche (Retired)
Atlanta

TONY CAMPBELL
President, Broadstreet Group
Thomasville

JOHN DOWNS
Senior Vice President of Public Affairs,
Coca-Cola Enterprises
Atlanta

JENNIFER GIFFEN
Vice President of Human Resources &
Services, GulfStream
Savannah

JEFF HERRIN
Vice President of Operations, Southwire
Carrollton

NEIL HIGHTOWER
President, Community Enterprises
Thomaston

PATRICK JONES
Executive Vice President,
Journey Productions
Atlanta

MARIO MARTINEZ
Managing Partner, Tecnix LLC
Alpharetta

CONSULTANTS: NORTH HIGHLAND

DEAN DELLA BERNARDA
DAVID CONNER
BOB CUCCHI
DAVE PETERSON
JIM POLAUKIS
DREW SCHRADER

KPMG

DON CARTER

FLEET MANAGEMENT I & II | 2004

I CHAIR: DON BURDESHAW
Director of Fleet Management,
Georgia Power (Retired)
Gardendale, AL

MARION BEACHAM
Transportation Manager, Shaw Industries
Dalton

TIFFANY CALLAWAY-FERRELL
LNG Operations Manager,
AGL Resources
Atlanta

BILL HIGHTOWER
Assistant Vice President, Network
Services, Logistics, BellSouth
Atlanta

KEN LEE
Vice President of International Security,
United Parcel Service
Atlanta

KEN QUIGG
Director of Logistics, Flowers Foods
Thomasville

CONSULTANT: BEARING POINT

AARON ESTIS

II CHAIR: ALBERT WRIGHT
Vice President of Engineering,
United Parcel Service
Atlanta

FRANK ARGENBRIGHT
Chairman, AirServ Corporation
Atlanta

JOHN BENTON
CFO, Peeples Industries
Savannah

RON KIRBY
Vice President of Fleet Operations,
United Parcel Service
Atlanta

RANDY MANEY
Fleet Operations Manager, Fieldale Farms
Baldwin

WILLIAM POPE
Pope Trucking
Douglas

CHIP WHITE
Executive Director, Logistics Institute
Georgia Tech
Atlanta

CONSULTANTS: UNITED PARCEL SERVICE

DANIEL O'DWYER
GEORGE WALTHER

PROCUREMENT | 2004

CHAIR: JIM BALLOUN
Chairman and CEO, Acuity Brands, Inc.
Atlanta

JIM BOSTIC
Executive Vice President, Georgia Pacific
Atlanta

JOHN CAMPI
Vice President, Global Sourcing,
The Home Depot
Atlanta

KEN CARTY
Director, Procurement,
The Coca-Cola Company
Atlanta

RUSSELL GRIZZLE
President, Milliken Floor Covering
LaGrange

ANITA HAYMAN
Procurement Manager, NutraSweet
Augusta

GEORGE LOTTIER
Executive Director, Georgia Minority
Supplier Development Council
Atlanta

JEFFREY ROLSTEN
Executive Director, Sourcing, Bell South
Atlanta

PAM TAMASI
Director, Corporate Services,
Scientific Atlanta
Lawrenceville

WILL VEREEN
Corporate Vice President,
Riverside Manufacturing
Moultrie

**CONSULTANTS: MCKINSEY &
COMPANY**
HANNAH CHOI
KEVIN COYNE
ANDY EVERSBUSCH
CHIP HARDT
AMY MULKEY

STRATEGIC INDUSTRIES | 2004

CHAIR: DAVID GARRETT III
Chairman, Mallory & Evans
Development
Atlanta

JAMES CHAVEZ
President, Tift County Chamber of
Commerce
Tifton

GEORGE ISRAEL
CEO, Georgia Chamber of Commerce
Atlanta

MELVIN KRUGER
CEO, L.E. Schwartz & Son, Inc.
Macon

FRANCIS LOTT
CEO, Lott Properties, Inc.
Douglas

JIMMY TALLENT
President, United Community Bank
Blairsville

ARNOLD TENENBAUM
Retired CEO, Chatham Steel
Savannah

JOANNE WALTER
President, WalterPan
Blue Ridge

HARIETTE WATKINS
AGL Resources
Atlanta

CONSULTANTS

BARBARA STAFFORD
GT INTERESTS
WILL HEARN
UNIVERSITY OF GEORGIA

COMPETITIVENESS | 2004

CHAIR: DWIGHT EVANS
Executive Vice President of External
Affairs, Southern Company
Atlanta

CAROLYN EAGER
Broker, Smith Barney
Valdosta

KELLY GAY
Chairman, President, CEO,
KnowledgeStorm
Atlanta

JOHN GORNALL
Partner, Arnall, Golden, & Gregory
Atlanta

DAVID LUCKIE
Executive Director, Griffin-Spalding
County Development Authority
Griffin

LYNN PITTS
Senior Vice President, Savannah
Economic Development Authority
Savannah

JOHN RIPOLL
Managing Director, Jackson Securities
Atlanta

CHARLES TARBUTTON
Vice President, Sandersville Railroad
Company
Sandersville

CONSULTANTS: ERNST & YOUNG

ROSE BURDEN
ROBERT HENDERSON
ERIC LANGE

ROBIN SPRATLIN
Manager, Economic Development Team,
Georgia Power
Atlanta

WORKFORCE DEVELOPMENT | 2004

CHAIR: ANN CRAMER
Director, Corporate Community
Relations, IBM Corporation
Atlanta

CONSULTANTS: IBM
GREG CHOUINIERE
BRIAN KRAMER
MARCELO ROMAN
LEE TORRENCE

CHARLES ASENSIO
Vice President, ADP Tax Services
Atlanta

BEN BOSWELL
Community Affairs Manager,
Wachovia Bank
Atlanta

JIM BUNTIN
Vice President,
Synovus Service Corporation
Columbus

DALE JONES
Managing Partner, Heidrick & Struggles
Atlanta

JEFF LUKKEN
Mayor, City of LaGrange
LaGrange

STEVE RIECK
Executive Director, Regional Leadership
Forum, Georgia State University
Atlanta

JOSEPHINE TAN
Georgia Power Company
Atlanta

AUDREY TILLMAN
Senior Vice President, Human Resources,
AFLAC
Columbus

JACK WARD
CEO, Russell Corporation
Atlanta

ACCOUNTS RECEIVABLE | 2005

CHAIR: DONNA HYLAND
President and CEO of Children's
Healthcare of Atlanta
Atlanta

FRANK ASKEW
Washington EMC
Sandersville

PHILLIP FAIRCLOTH
Farmer's Furniture
Dublin

HARRY GOLDBERG
BellSouth
Atlanta

DAVID HANNA
CompuCredit
Atlanta

DON HEROMAN
Equifax
Atlanta

JERRY NIX
Genuine Parts
Atlanta

KRIS NORDHOLZ
Wilheit Packaging
Gainesville

ANN STALLARD
Graphic Communications
Lawrenceville

LYNN WENTWORTH
BellSouth
Atlanta

CONSULTANTS: KPMG

DAVE DENNIS
DAVID ROBERTS
PAUL STEPUSIN

PUBLIC FINANCE OPTIONS | 2005

CHAIR: PHIL HUMANN
Chairman, President and CEO, SunTrust
Atlanta

PIN PIN CHAU
CEO, Summit National Bank
Atlanta

TOM COLEY
Vice Chair, SouthTrust Bank
Birmingham, AL

TOM FANNING
Executive Vice President & CFO,
Southern Company
Atlanta

JOHN HUNTZ
Managing Director, Fuqua Ventures
Atlanta

MATT NICHOLS
Partner, Sutherland, Asbill, & Brennan
Atlanta

DAVID SJOQUIST
Professor, Georgia State University
Atlanta

BOB STEED
Retired Partner, King & Spalding LLP
Atlanta

RICHARD WOODARD
King & Spalding LLP
Atlanta

JIM YOUNG
President and CEO, Citizens Trust Bank
Atlanta

**CONSULTANTS: GOLDMAN
SACHS & CO.**

RICK FITZGERALD
JUSTIN GOLDSTEIN

COMMUNITY CARE FOR BEHAVIORAL HEALTH AND DEVELOPMENTAL DISABILITIES | 2005

CHAIR: BRUCE COOK
Founder, President and CEO
Choosing the Best Publishing
Atlanta

JIM BECK
Director, Government Relations/Public
Affairs, Nationwide Insurance Co.
Carrollton

LYNNETTE BRAGG
Chair, Governor's Council on
Developmental Disabilities
Springfield

DR. PETER BUCKLEY
Chair, Department of Psychiatry &
Health Behavior, Medical College of
Georgia
Augusta

BECKY BUTLER
Consultant, Annie E. Casey Foundation
Atlanta

ANN CRAMER
Director, Corporate Community
Relations, IBM Corporation
Atlanta

BOB FINK
CEO, Ridgeview Institute
Smyrna

JUDY FITZGERALD
Project Coordinator,
Atlanta Business Leaders Initiatives
Mableton

ED GRAVES
Chair, Governor's Advisory Council for
MHMRSA
Cedartown

DAVID LUSHBAUGH
President, NAMI Georgia
Atlanta

ANNA MCLAUGHLIN
Co-Chief Executive Officer,
Georgia Parent Support Network
Atlanta

ANN PARKER PH.D.
VP Human Resources & Corporate
Psychologist, Waffle House
Atlanta

SHERRY TUCKER
Executive Director, Georgia Mental
Health Consumer Network
Decatur

CARLIS WILLIAMS
Organization: Regional Administrator,
Administration for Children & Families
Atlanta

CUSTOMER SERVICE | 2005

CHAIR: JOE DOYLE
Administrator, Governor's Office of
Consumer Affairs
Atlanta

TIM BURGESS
Department of Community Health
Atlanta

JERRI CLOUD
The University of Georgia
Atlanta

TOM DANIEL
Board of Regents
Atlanta

GREG DOZIER
Department of Driver Services
Atlanta

JOY HAWKINS
Governor's Office
Atlanta

LES HOLLINGSWORTH
Department of Economic Development
Atlanta

NOEL HOLCOMB
Department of Natural Resources
Atlanta

BOB NEWSOME
Department of Natural Resources
Atlanta

KAY ROBINSON
Constituent Services, Office of the
Governor
Atlanta

BILL ROPER
Joe Tanner and Associates
Atlanta

RON STARK
Board of Regents, University System of
Georgia
Atlanta

CAROL VEIHMEYER
Georgia Technology Authority
Atlanta

DANA RUSSELL
Department of Administrative Services
Atlanta

MIKE VOLLMER
Department of Technical and Adult
Education
Atlanta

TOM WADE
Georgia Technology Authority
Atlanta

B. J. WALKER
Department of Human Resources
Atlanta

RICHARD YOUNG
Office of Planning and Budget
Atlanta

STATE HEALTH BENEFITS | 2005

CO-CHAIR: BILL WALLACE
Associate Vice Chancellor for Human
Resources, Board of Regents,
University System of Georgia
Atlanta

CO-CHAIR: ELLEN LINDEMANN
Senior Vice President of Human
Resources, Southern Company
Atlanta

ROBERT BELL
Southern Company
Atlanta

ILEANA CONNALLY
Vice President of Benefits, Home Depot
Atlanta

BARBARA GILBREATH
Director, Global Employee Benefits &
Programs, The Coca-Cola Company
Atlanta

GELANE HAMILTON
Organization: Director of Operations,
State Benefit Plan Division, Department
of Community Health
Atlanta

JODY HUNTER
Senior Director of Benefits,
Georgia Pacific
Atlanta

GEORGE ISRAEL
CEO, Georgia Chamber of Commerce
Atlanta

DONNA LANGE
Senior Vice President for Corporate
Benefits, SunTrust
Atlanta

ABEL ORTIZ
Governor's Office
Atlanta

KATE PFIRMAN
Office of Planning and Budget
Atlanta

MELANIE PLATT
Senior Vice President, Human Resources,
AGL Resources
Atlanta

MARY STRANGER
Director of Benefits, Synovus
Columbus

DALE WHITNEY
Corporate Health and Welfare Manager,
United Parcel Service
Atlanta

TERRY WOMACK
Staff Vice President, Human Resources,
Bell South
Atlanta

**CONSULTANTS: HEWITT
ASSOCIATES LLC**
ANDY HILES
MICHAEL MAROTTA
GARY SETTERBERG

RISK MANAGEMENT | 2006

CHAIR: LARRY GAUNT, PH.D.
Professor Emeritus of Risk Management
and Insurance, Georgia State University
Atlanta

J. GARY MEGGS
Director of Risk Management,
Southern Company Services, Inc.
Atlanta

DAVID A. PAULK
Director of Risk Management,
Association of County Commissioners of
Georgia
Atlanta

ART KIRCHOFFER
Executive Director, Risk Management,
AT&T (BellSouth)
Atlanta

AVIATION | 2006

CHAIR: RANDY HUDON
Executive Director, Corporate Aviation &
Travel Services BellSouth
Atlanta

STEVE PARLIAMENT
SE Region Transportation Manager,
United Parcel Service
Atlanta

GEOFF BURKART
Director, Aircraft Maintenance & Security
Director BellSouth
Atlanta

NEAL PURCELL
Retired Partner, KPMG
Atlanta

DON CLEVENGER
Aviation Dept Manager,
Southern Company
Atlanta

MIKE SCHELLER
Aviation Director, Aflac
Columbus

TONEY FRANK
District Air Manager,
United Parcel Service
Atlanta

DAVID SMALL
Chair, Fleet Operations Administrator,
Georgia Business Aviation Association,
Cox Enterprises
Atlanta

BILL KAHLE
General Manager, Corporate Aviation,
The Coca Cola Company
Atlanta

JOHN SMITH
Chief Pilot, Waffle House
Atlanta

HENRY LOWE
President, Lowe Aviation
Macon

LANCE TOLAND
President, Lance Toland Assoc.
Griffin

**CONSULTANT: OFFICE OF
PLANNING & BUDGET**

RICHARD YOUNG

SERVICE DELIVERY | 2007

CHAIR: PAUL WOOD
President and Chief Executive Officer,
Georgia Electric Membership Corporation
Tucker

MIKE BEATTY
Commissioner, Department of
Community Affairs
Atlanta

MELVIN DAVIS
Chair, Oconee County Board of
Commissioners
Watkinsville

JIM DOVE
Executive Director, Northeast Georgia
Regional Development Centers
Athens

EUGENE DYAL
Chair, Bacon County Board of
Commissioners
Alma

PAT GRAHAM
Mayor, City of Braselton
Braselton

EARL LEONARD JR.
Senior Vice President of Public Affairs,
The Coca Cola Company (Retired)
Atlanta

BERNARD REYNOLDS
Georgia Electric Membership Corporation
Atlanta

GAYE SMITH
Former Director, Family Connection
Partnership
Athens

RON STEPHENS
Representative, Georgia House of
Representatives
Savannah

LARRY WALKER
Attorney-at-Law, Walker, Hulbert, Gray
& Byrd
Perry

JOHN WILES
Senator, Georgia State Senate
Marietta

CHRISTOPHER WOMACK
Executive Vice President of External
Affairs, Georgia Power Company
Atlanta

WILLIAM YEARTA
Mayor, City of Sylvester
Sylvester

TRANSPORTATION | 2007

CHAIR: NEAL PURCELL
Partner, KPMG (Retired)
Atlanta

DR. DAVID ALLEN
Chair, Georgia Chamber of Commerce
Atlanta

ROBERT L. BROWN
President & CEO, R. L. Brown &
Associates, Inc.
Atlanta

BEN HALL
President and CEO, Dublin Construction
Company
Dublin

EDWARD S. HEYS JR.
Atlanta Deputy Managing Partner,
Deloitte & Touche LLP
Atlanta

DR. MICHAEL D. MEYER
Professor of Civil and Environmental
Engineering, Georgia Institute of
Technology
Atlanta

SAM OLENS
Chairman, Cobb County Board of
Commissioners
Marietta

SUZANNE SITHERWOOD
President, Atlanta Gas Light
Atlanta

TOMMY STALNAKER
Director of Operations, Houston County
Public Works
Perry

CONSULTANTS: DELOITTE CONSULTING LLP
MARK PIGHINI
JOHN CIARAMELLA JR.
TOM WALKER
JOHN CULLIAN

OFFICE OF PLANNING AND BUDGET
KRISTINA STROEDE

FREIGHT AND LOGISTICS | 2007

CHAIR: ROBERT J. FAULS JR.
President and Owner,
Southern Freight, Inc.
Atlanta

RAYBON ANDERSON
Board Member, Georgia DOT
Statesboro

TOM ARMSTRONG
Director of Strategic Development,
Georgia Ports Authority
Savannah

RUDY BOWEN
Board Member, Georgia DOT
Duluth

CHRISTIAN FISCHER
Executive Vice President, Packaging,
Georgia-Pacific LLC
Atlanta

CHERYL FULGINITI
Vice President, Engineering,
United Parcel Service
Atlanta

MARK HOLIFIELD
Senior Vice President, Global Supply
Chain, The Home Depot
Atlanta

WARREN JONES
Aviation Development Manager,
Hartsfield-Jackson Atlanta International
Airport
Atlanta

JEFF MULLIS
Senator, Georgia State Senate
Chickamauga

NEEL SHAH
Vice President of Cargo, Delta Airlines
Atlanta

VANCE SMITH
Representative, Georgia House of
Representatives
Pine Mountain

EDWARD SUTTER
Vice President, Supply Chain,
Coca-Cola Enterprises
Atlanta

**LEAD CONSULTANT: GEORGIA
LOGISTICS INNOVATION CENTER**
PAGE SIPLON
Executive Director

**CONSULTANTS:
BOOZ|ALLEN|HAMILTON**
JANNETT THOMS
ROBBY MOSS

COMMERCIALIZATION/INTELLECTUAL PROPERTY | 2008

CHAIR: RICHARD USSERY,
Chairman of the Board, TSYS
Columbus

MARK ALLEN
Vice President of Research, Georgia Tech
Atlanta

FRED COOPER
Cooper Capital
Atlanta

ERROLL DAVIS
Chancellor, University System of Georgia
Atlanta

STEVEN FLEMING
ATDC
Atlanta

DAVID LEE
Vice President of Research,
University of Georgia
Athens

HERB LEHMAN
Georgia Department of Economic
Development
Atlanta

DAVID RATCLIFFE
President and CEO, Southern Company
Atlanta

KEN STEWART
Commissioner, Georgia Department of
Economic Development
Atlanta

TOM CALLAWAY
Life Science Partners
Atlanta

CONSULTANT: KAUFFMAN FOUNDATION
LESA MITCHELL

RECRUITMENT, RETENTION, RETIREMENT | 2008

CHAIR: BILL WALLACE
Associate Vice Chancellor for Human
Resources (Retired), Board of Regents,
University System of Georgia
Atlanta

SHARON DOUGLAS
Vice President, Chief People Officer,
Human Resource Services, Aflac
Columbus

ROBERT DUNN
Senior Vice President, Human Resources,
Mueller Water Products, Inc.
Atlanta

MARION FEDRICK
Assistant Commissioner, Total Rewards,
State Personnel Administration
Atlanta

BILL HEATH
Chair, Senate Retirement Committee,
Georgia State Senate
Atlanta

MICHAEL JOHNSON
United State Operations Human
Resources Coordinator,
United Parcel Services
Atlanta

ELLEN LINDEMANN
Senior Vice President, Human Resources
(Retired), Southern Company
Atlanta

LINDA MATZIGKEIT
Senior Vice President, Human Resources,
Children's Healthcare of Atlanta
Atlanta

HOWARD MAXWELL
Vice Chair, House Retirement
Committee, Georgia House of
Representatives
Atlanta

LEE RUDD
Deputy Commissioner, Operations and
Workforce Services, State Personnel
Administration
Atlanta

ROBERT WARD
Senior Vice President, Corporate Services,
Synovus
Columbus

**CONSULTANTS: HEWITT
ASSOCIATES LLC**
ANDY HILES
GARY SETTERBERG
SALEM SHUNNARAH

PATTI BAILEY
Member, State Personnel Board

STATE INVESTMENT STRATEGIES | 2009

CHAIR: WENDELL STARKE
Principal, Willis Investment Counsel
Gainesville

HUGH ALBRITTON III
Chair & CEO, Albritton Management
Capital
Alpharetta

MARY CAHILL
Emory University
Atlanta

AL GASIOREK
Chief Investment Officer, Children's
Healthcare of Atlanta
Atlanta

CHARLES MOSELEY
Partner, Noro-Moseley
Board Member, Teachers Retirement
System of Georgia
Atlanta

FRANCES ROGERS
President, Checks & Balances, Inc.
Atlanta

JIM TAYLOR
Chief Investment Officer, Georgia Tech
Foundation, Inc.
Atlanta

J. ALVIN WILBANKS
Superintendent, Gwinnett County
Schools,
Board Member, Employee Retirement
System of Georgia
Lawrenceville

NED WINSOR
Assistant Treasurer, United Parcel Services
Vice Chairman, Employee Retirement
System of Georgia
Atlanta

APPENDIX D

KEY PLAYERS ON THE TRANSFORMATION TEAM

GOVERNOR'S EXECUTIVE LEADERSHIP

ERIC TANENBLATT	Chief of Staff, 2003
JOHN WATSON	Chief of Staff, 2003-2008
ED HOLCOMBE	Chief of Staff, 2008-2011
JIM LIENTZ	Chief Operating Officer 2003-2010
TOMMY HILLS	Chief Financial Officer 2003-2011
TREY CHILDRESS	Chief Operating Officer 2010-2011

ENTERPRISE AGENCY LEADERSHIP

BRAD DOUGLAS	Commissioner, Department of Administrative Services
STEVE STEVENSON	Commissioner, State Personnel Administration
PATRICK MOORE	Executive Director, Georgia Technology Authority, and State Chief Information Officer
GENA ABRAHAM	State Property Commissioner, 2004-2007
STEVEN STANCIL	State Property Commissioner, 2007-2011
JOE DOYLE	Administrator, Office of Consumer Affairs, Office of Customer Service
LYNN VELLINGA	State Accounting Officer 2004-2008
GREG GRIFFIN	State Accounting Officer – 2008-2011
BART GRAHAM	Commissioner, Department of Revenue 2003-2010

GOVERNOR'S OFFICE OF IMPLEMENTATION

LONICE BARRETT	Director, 2004-2006
SID JOHNSON	Director 2006-2007
JEFF STRANE	Director 2007-2010

COMMISSION FOR A NEW GEORGIA
EXECUTIVE AND MANAGING STAFF

BILL TODD — Executive Director, 2003
ANNIE HUNT BURRISS — Executive Director, 2003-2005
KRIS NORDHOLZ — Deputy Executive Director, 2003-2004
JERRY GUTHRIE — Managing Director, 2004-2009
SHARON MCMAHON — Manager of Strategic Information Services 2004-2010
BRENDA WISE — Program Coordinator, 2003-2005
SHERRY LYLE — Program Coordinator, 2005-2008

COMMISSION FOR A NEW GEORGIA INTERNS AND *FELLOWS

MARY ALEXANDER
*JESSE BLAND
DAVID R. CANNON
LISA CUPID
STACEY ESTERMAN
*MELISSA HELSBY
*PETER HYLTON
TALMADGE INFINGER
TYLER INFINGER
BRIANA JAMES
SAMUEL JOYNER

*LAURA JOHNSON
LAUREN KLEIN
DAVID LEBLANG
EDMUND MCAFEE
MEGAN MCCARTER
*DAVID OZBURN
PHILLIP RUBIN
ANDY WITCHER
JULIA WOODWARD
HARRY WOODWORTH

APPENDIX E

LEGISLATION FOR A BEST-MANAGED STATE

HB 1195 (2010) WORKFORCE DEVELOPMENT

SPONSORS: REPS.TERRY ENGLAND, JIMMY PRUETT, CLAY COX, MELVIN EMERSON, MIKE COAN, SEN. CHIP PEARSON

Created the Workforce Investment Board and membership make-up and established the Governor's Office of Workforce Development to implement state workforce development policy as directed by the governor. The act recognizes the 'Georgia Work Ready' as the state's branded workforce development enterprise.

HB 867 (2010) REGIONAL COMMISSIONS

SPONSORS: REP. RON STEPHENS / SEN. TOMMIE WILLIAMS

Increased accountability of the district Regional Commissions (RCs) to their local governments and the state, requiring regular financial and performance audits. Minimum levels of financial participation are set for state and local partners. By law, RCs will focus on four core planning areas: land use, transportation, environmental protection and historic preservation. The law is designed to ensure that all local governments throughout the State have access to quality assistance across those functions.

HB 371 (2009) RETIREMENT INVESTMENT

SPONSORS: REP. EARL EHRHART / SEN. KASIM REED

Amended the "Public Retirement Systems Investment Authority Law" to increase allowable retirement system fund investment in equities to 75 percent.

SB 230 (2009) COMMUNITY SERVICE BOARDS AND MENTAL HEALTH SERVICES

SPONSOR: SEN. CURT THOMPSON

Transferred the duties relating to the administration of mental health, mental retardation, substance abuse, and other disability services to the Department of Human Resources.

SB 85 (2009) Georgia Aviation Authority

SPONSORS: SENS. BILL HEATH, BILL COWSERT, CHIP PEARSON, JIM BUTTERWORTH, ROSS TOLLESON, RONNIE CHANCE

Created the Georgia Aviation Authority to govern the state's aircraft management. The aviation authority will deploy aircraft to meet the missions of multiple agencies with fewer aircraft, standardize types of aircraft, modernize the fleet and establish a unified team of aviation professionals to ensure safe, effective and efficient operations.

HB 1113 (2008) Penalties for personal use of state purchasing

SPONSORS: REPS. JOHN HEARD, ED RYNDERS, PENNY HOUSTON, GREG MORRIS, RICHARD ROYAL, GERALD GREENE / SEN. MITCH SEABAUGH

Codified penalties for personal use of state purchasing resources, including P-cards, purchase orders, contracts, and credit, charge or debit cards.

HB 1216 (2008) Regional Development Centers

SPONSORS: REPS. RON STEPHENS, VANCE SMITH, JOE WILKINSON, GENE MADDOX, JOHN LUNSFORD, BARBARA SIMS, SEN. TOMMIE WILLIAMS

Changed regional development centers to Regional Commissions and created new boundaries, membership and authority to audit. Set duties and procedures for regional commissions' relationships with other governmental entities.

SB 425 (2008) Risk Management

SPONSOR: SEN. JOHNNY GRANT

Authorized the Risk Management Services Division to establish incentive programs to reduce risk, including differential premium rates and deductibles based on loss histories of state agencies, institutions and authorities, and such entities' participation in loss control programs.

SB 592 (2008) Surplus sales

SPONSORS: SENS. JOHNNY GRANT, JACK HILL, BRIAN KEMP, SETH HARP

Authorized the Department of Administrative Services to sell small value surplus equipment and other property, turned in by state agencies, to the public at retail warehouses, increasing citizen access to surplus bargains.

HB 312 (2005) ADMINISTRATIVE SERVICES & PROCUREMENT

SPONSORS: REP. ALLEN FREEMAN, SEN. CASEY CAGLE

Initiated changes to transform the state's procurement function and improve the management of the state's assets, including motor vehicles. The legislation provides incentives for surplus property enhancements, strengthens policy leadership over the state's motor vehicle fleet and streamlines personal property inventory procedures.

SB 158 (2005) CAPITAL ASSET MANAGEMENT

SPONSORS: SEN. JIM WHITEHEAD, REP. TERRY BARNARD

Provided for the comprehensive revision of provisions regarding state property for consolidation and effective management of the rental of administrative space and the acquisition, use, and disposition of real property by the state and state authorities. The act transferred authority for property management to the State Properties Commission, including assets, contracts, leases, inventory and management of administrative space and compiling information on all state facilities.

SB 125 (2005) NEW GEORGIA FOUNDATION FOR TOURISM ACT

SPONSORS: SEN. JEFF MULLIS / REP. VANCE SMITH

Created the New Georgia Foundation for Tourism to coordinate marketing efforts and consolidate funding to improve the promotion of the State's tourism resources. Also coordinated administration by assigning the four Halls of Fame to the Department of Economic Development.

HB 275 (2005) DEFERRED COMPENSATION TRANSFER

SPONSORS: REP. JIM COLE / SEN. CHIP ROGERS

Transferred the employee-deferred compensation programs to the Employees' Retirement System from the Georgia Merit System, consolidating administration and expertise in one location.

HB 293 (2005) State Accounting Office

SPONSORS: REP. LARRY O'NEAL / SEN. CASEY CAGLE

Created Georgia's first State Accounting Office to realign the state's financial reporting and financial system responsibilities under a single State Accounting Officer (SAO). In 2006, Georgia met the deadline for the annual federal audit report for the first time since 1991.

HB 501 (2005) Department of Drivers Services

SPONSORS: REPS. AUSTIN SCOTT, ROSS TOLLESON

Created the Department of Drivers Services as a successor agency to the Department of Motor Vehicle Safety to provide for vehicle safety and responsibility for driver's licensing services. This was the first statewide initiative to improve services to citizens.

HB 191 (2005) Allocation Formula

SPONSORS: REPS. LARRY O'NEAL, ROGER WILLIAMS / SEN. CASEY CAGLE

Improved allocation and apportionment formulas for corporations in order to provide economic incentives for businesses to invest in employment growth and capital projects in the state.

HB 389 (2005) Tax Credits for Less Developed Counties

SPONSORS: REPS. JAY ROBERTS, RICHARD SMITH, VANCE SMITH, JON BURNS, RICH GOLICK, JEFF MAY, SEN. CASEY CAGLE.

Provided tax credits for creation of jobs paying higher than average and offering access to health insurance, applying to less-developed counties in the state.

HB 509 (2005) Revenue Shortfall Reserve

SPONSORS: REPS. BEN HARBIN, JERRY KEEN, MARK BURKHALTER, SEN. JACK HILL

Doubled the maximum level of the contribution to the Revenue Shortfall Reserve from five percent of the prior year's revenues to 10 percent. Designated surplus state funds are added each fiscal year and carry forward from fiscal year to fiscal year to cover expenditures exceeding revenue.

APPENDIX E

TASK FORCE RECOMMENDATIONS

ENTERPRISE MANAGEMENT

ADMINISTRATIVE SERVICES

- Realign Administrative Services by function to promote clear policy making, stronger accountability and customer focus.
- Make State Purchasing more efficient and service-driven through e-procurement with strategic sourcing.
- Consolidate Human Resource activities common to all state organizations.
- Refocus Georgia Technology Authority to enact its mission to develop and promote IT planning, implementation and management.
- Implement a new statewide Asset Management Program integrated with the state's financial and purchasing system.

PROCUREMENT

- Establish a single center-leading purchasing agent to most efficiently purchase all goods and services for the State
- Set criteria to determine when purchases are made centrally or left to the individual agencies.

ASSET MANAGEMENT

FLEET MANAGEMENT I & II

- Broaden Existing Fleet Management.
- Track Ownership Costs.
- Centralize Fleet Management.
- New vehicle assignment and commuting policy.

AVIATION

- Consolidate leadership and operations.
- Align the fleet, facilities and missions.
- Establish state-wide standards.
- Establish a consolidated fleet and facility plan and planning process.
- Refurbish the Economic Development Gateway (Fulton County Airport facility).
- Eliminate all federal surplus aircraft.

- Establish a user billing process to recoup all costs.
- Establish coordinated aircraft scheduling with leadership team oversight.
- Engage with industry and trade organizations.

PROPERTY MANAGEMENT
SPACE MANAGEMENT

- Establish a real estate entity to manage all state-owned and leased property.
- Consolidate leases to reduce costs.
- Identify surplus land and buildings, and utilize or sell to reduce costs.
- Assess property holdings through an inventory of current information on all real estate.
- Use portfolio management strategies and tools for effective decision-making.

CAPITAL CONSTRUCTION

- Establish a State Property Officer with responsibility for all capital construction.
- Develop a clear mission, vision and guiding principles for capital construction and property management.
- Evaluate real estate assets for reallocation and opportunities to sell.
- Reallocate General Obligation (G.O.) Bonds no longer needed due to canceled or completed projects.
- Develop statewide protocols – policies, procedures and tools – to manage capital construction services.

FINANCIAL MANAGEMENT
PUBLIC FINANCE OPTIONS

- Take planning measures to protect the state's AAA credit ratings.
- Revise State Constitution to allow state-of-the-art financial tools and techniques and maximum flexibility.
- Improve debt management practices and strategies to lower borrowing costs, manage risk, and achieve greater financial flexibility and efficiency.
- Leverage conduit issuers to issue revenue bonds on behalf of the State.
- Support private equity to increase pension fund returns, mitigate portfolio risk, create jobs, spur innovation and offer citizens new services.

ACCOUNTS RECEIVABLE

- Develop a statewide policy on receivables/collections with a monitoring program.
- Seek legislation and programmatic changes to aid statewide collection.
- Seek legislation to establish Chief Financial Officer and Chief Accounting Officer.
- Track delinquent receivables.
- Reassign Department of Community Health's Prospective Payment Program.

- Develop and implement cash management policies and consolidate accounts.
- Provide departmental collection forecasts to predict cash flow and monitor collections.

STATE INVESTMENT STRATEGIES

- Liberalize the asset allocation guidelines currently set by the state to include authorizing new investment options.
- Engage an external organization to monitor performance on a periodic basis.
- Permit selection of external managers based on investment criteria alone.
- Salary ranges and incentive pay for senior staff should continue to be reviewed annually to retain and recruit professional staff as alternative assets are added.
- Clarify in a statement the process by which trading order is determined by managers to ensure SEC trading rules are consistently being observed.

COST MANAGEMENT
RISK MANAGEMENT

- Reorganize the Risk Management Services (RMS) division with fewer, higher level, professional managers supported by technically qualified staff.
- Revise the cost allocation system to create a more responsive, equitable and incentive based method of funding.
- Create a comprehensive set of performance measures that are meaningful and accurate as a management tool.
- Create the position of loss control manager within the RMS Division.
- Expand the understanding and use of actuarial analysis by RMS.
- Examine the inter-agency process of managing claims in litigation.

STATE HEALTH BENEFITS

- Improve the decision-making process.
- Upgrade operations and structure.
- Improve design efficiency.
- Restructure retiree medical program.
- Provide a simple, low cost, limited choice option.
- Move to greater levels of health care consumerism.

ECONOMIC GROWTH
TOURISM

- Consolidate Georgia's tourism efforts into a single, independent authority.
- Evaluate the goals and performance of each organization supporting tourism, and determine a long-term strategy for the overall tourism effort.
- Expand public and private funding for tourism marketing, advertising and research.

- Develop a master development plan for Coastal Georgia.
- Review current incentives to promote tourism jobs and investment.
- Support legislation enabling the Georgia Department of Economic Development to join the private sector in tourism marketing efforts.

STRATEGIC INDUSTRIES

- Focus economic development efforts on growing the following industries in Georgia: Aerospace, Agribusiness, Energy and Environment, Healthcare and Eldercare, Life Sciences and, Logistics and Transportation.
- Establish a statewide, centralized commercialization center as the point of contact for research and commercialization opportunities.
- Coordinate economic development efforts through the Governor to focus consistently on Georgia's strategic plan for economic development.
- Establish a university-affiliated Research Park.

COMPETITIVENESS

- Create Governor's Cabinet for Economic and Workforce Development, comprising relevant agency heads to coordinate the state's prospect process.
- Focus financial incentives on industries as strategic to Georgia's growth.
- Develop a plan to recruit and retain business investors, ideas and research in Georgia.

WORKFORCE DEVELOPMENT

- Establish a private, non-profit workforce development corporation and staff accountable for the success of Georgia's workforce development efforts.
- Aggregate or create a set of processes and technology solutions that enables the success of the WFD system objectives.
- Support and enable the Georgia Education Community's (pre-k through 16) efforts to consistently generate or retrain workers with skills employers need.
- Improve the existing WFD system to make it more dynamic, resilient, and able to drive and sustain future economic growth.
- Implement an effective communications plan to ensure that all employers and citizens understand, can use and embrace the WFD system.

COMMERCIALIZATION/INTELLECTUAL PROPERTY

- The University System should invest, provide and maintain standardized enterprise-wide innovation management software system to its research universities.
- Develop an enterprise-wide structure which recognizes the importance of research accomplishments within the University System.
- Create system-wide vehicle to promote and integrate "best practice" education and process improvement within the research universities.
- Establish a mechanism or an advisory group at the enterprise level to encourage and facilitate the development of an open innovation system.

- Establish at the enterprise level an ongoing marketing program which creates and leverages the enterprise data into a Georgia marketplace.

FREIGHT AND LOGISTICS

- Identify and market Georgia's differentiating logistics advantages.
- Establish a statewide Freight Mobility Information Exchange.
- Identify, establish and promote statewide freight corridors and hubs.
- Promote and support workforce, training, and educational programs.
- Conduct an inventory of all public and private rail assets in the State.
- Develop a demand driven strategic statewide freight and logistics plan.
- Make future infrastructure plans more durable.
- Create a supportive business model.
- Establish a focused freight-and-logistics division within the Department of Transportation (GDOT).

TRANSPORTATION / RETURN ON INVESTMENT

- Pre-purchase key material commodities to "lock-in" select prices.
- Monitor material prices and space projects to avoid peak demand
- Decrease timeframe to secure ROW with incentives to expedite acquisition.
- Bundle or split projects to attract out-of-state or attract smaller, local contractors.
- Coordinate efforts.
- Increase transparency and accountability.
- Reduce silos.
- Consider completing Value Engineering studies for projects under $25 million.
- Increase flexibility of specs in GDOT's current life-cycle cost/benefit analysis design.
- Consider alternate materials or construction that reduce cost and maintain quality.
- Develop a "Partnering Approach" with the consulting and contracting community.
- Shorten the timeframe for fulfilling federal project requirements, to improve delivery.
- Drive performance metrics to better monitor and report on key cost and schedule parameters and increase transparency and accountability in the project life-cycle.
- Maximize the use of design-build where appropriate.
- Request GDOT to work with a small group of contractors and consultants to encourage a partnering relationship that will improve operations.

CULTURE OF SERVICE

LEADERSHIP DEVELOPMENT

- Establish a state government executive leadership development program to train and prepare current and future State government leaders.

CUSTOMER SERVICE

- Start creating the culture and setting expectations for how we should serve our customers.
- Imbed process improvement and cultural development methodologies to drive continuous improvements.
- Create a general Information Call Center.
- Improve the performance of existing call handling services.
- Implement a Virtual Call Center (remote worker) program.

RECRUITMENT, RETENTION & RETIREMENT

- Develop an overarching plan to accelerate and coordinate the transformation of the state Human Resources function to act more as a single, multi-unit enterprise.
- Develop Statewide Employee Value Proposition (EVP) and align HR programs.
- Expand initiatives to brand and market the experience of working at the state.
- Divide the workforce during this transition, delivering Total Rewards value differently to each group.
- Make significant investments in decision-support and employee education.

SERVICE DELIVERY

SERVICE DELIVERY

- Replace Regional Development Centers with Regional Commissions, establishing new governance, funding and accountability structures.
- Incorporate proposed changes in 2008 legislation.
- Changes in board structure become effective July 1, 2008, in the coastal region.
- All other changes become effective July 1, 2009, including new Regional Commission boundaries.

COMMUNITY CARE FOR BEHAVIORAL HEALTH AND DEVELOPMENTAL DISABILITIES

- Establish a fee-for-service provider system.
- Require the use of evidence based/best outcome practices.
- Develop an open, competitive Community Service Bureau and provider environment.
- Establish greater accountability for outcomes and performance.
- Provide appropriate utilization of the state hospital system and reinvest saved dollars into community care.
- Establish a single System of Care for children and adolescents.
- Develop an effective intervention program for the MH/AD needs of the adult offender population.

ADDENDUM

It was to be expected: the book would be finished while the story goes on. This once-leftover blank page offered a space to slip three short updates under the wire at press-time.

SURPLUS PROPERTY SALES

In 2004, Georgia's three surplus warehouses were crammed with government cast-offs, from old police cars to school desks. The stuff was sold at thrift-store prices, often below the cost of overhead, and mostly to folks in neighboring communities. The warehouse operations were on a downhill trend as a money-loser for the state. That December, Governor Perdue directed the Surplus Property Division (SPD) to start posting used merchandise on eBay (pp. 89-90). Over three years, Georgia's virtual auction business took over all sales and evolved as one of the nation's first totally on-line markets for state surplus. The warehouses were shuttered. In July 2010, year-to-date sales surpassed $4.3 million, drawing buyers from 32 states and several countries via eBay, GovDeals and other web auctions. In 2010, SPD earned eBay's "Top-Rated Seller" status with a 99.6 customer satisfaction score. The division's innovative business model also won the Outstanding Program Award from the National Association of State Chief Administrators.

PROCUREMENT

In 2009, the Pew Center on the States selected Georgia's invention of a Spend Management Analytics tool – aka the procurement "spend cube"– as a Lab States Project (p. 132). Pew saw this revolutionary system for detecting and dissecting purchasing patterns and spending data as a national model that could be replicated by other states. Developers soon realized that the system had even broader value as a management tool, offering the ability to track and analyze state spending from all sources and budgetary angles in near-real time. To provide the program with a business intelligence platform, in 2010 Microsoft released software enabling the system to capture, refresh and visualize the precision analytics for strategic management of billions of dollars in state spending.

TRAVEL SERVICES

In 2010, the state began looking at the volume of state travel and how to leverage the $100 million spent annually on air, hotel and rental car expenses. The goal was to position the state in the travel market as a single employer versus 100-plus agencies individually procuring their own travel. The on-line system takes advantage of the best rates available and streamlines travel transactions end to end, from booking through expense reimbursement directly into the employee's paycheck.

ACKNOWLEDGEMENTS AND APPRECIATION

No book is an island, although it sometimes seems so to the writer surrounded by a sea of files, notebooks and flotsam of stray papers apropos to nothing. Writing a book is not a task to take on late or lightly. But that's how it's often done when its purpose is to preserve a record of a period of history at its closing. The moment comes to publish or perish. This is one of those books, and it would not be here without the essential contributions of many highly capable public servants, service-minded citizens, a dedicated pair of research assistants, and an editor and designer who did superb work under pressure.

Calling out names risks inadvertent omissions. Those who remain unsung can be sure that their efforts were recognized and appreciated in the acknowledgements that follow:

Pulling together the facts, commentary and detail necessary to describe the complexity of this subject matter can only be accomplished by pulling together as a team. The team which ultimately brought this record to print includes innumerable contributors who came through with reports and information on short notice at busy times. They are the administrators, managers and staff of more than a dozen state agencies which figured prominently in the transformation effort. Their expert and timely assistance was indispensible.

Corporate executives, government officials and consultants made time on their crowded calendars to be interviewed. Their observations and thoughts gave context and meaning to the clinical details of the process of re-engineering bureaucracy. Most of their names and comments appear through the book. Others who were not mentioned gave highly informative background which put this commission's effort in historical perspective of previous initiatives – which were equally impressive, but not equally implemented. All of these contributions were equally valuable, if not equally recognized.

The production of the book required significant work by research assistants who gathered facts, transcribed interviews, organized voluminous notebooks of materials and cherry-picked pages for index preparation. Two Governor's Fellows were instrumental in these essential tasks: Melissa Helsby, a graduate of Indiana University, and Laura Johnson, a graduate of East Tennessee State University.

THERE IS A SPECIAL PLACE in a writer's heart for the editor and designer who embrace the book as their own. Editorial and design work on a narrative constructed with such complicated and meticulous detail requires the talents of professionals who are masterfully skilled in their craft. It has been their challenge to interpret and organize miles of text and make it as clear and consumable as possible for the reader, both visually and editorially. This book has been the fortunate product of two such professionals whose work made all the difference in its quality:

Jeanne Potter is a superb and experienced editor and writer, who finds and fixes painful prose, punctuation pitfalls and problems the writer didn't even know were problems. Because she writes beautifully herself, she does not abide a lesser standard as an editor. Her dedication and pickiness resulted in many rescues from the gremlins of publishing that live forever on acid-free paper.

Daniel Fell is an excellent graphic designer who understands how to create a working relationship between words and layout. His intent – and at times insistence – was to create a visually clean, coherent and navigable flow of diverse elements within long stretches of narrative, designing focal points and breaks to keep everything from running together. His patience in dealing with too many changes – and then changing the changes – was remarkable.

Finally, this book truly would not be in print without the Mercer University Press. Director Marc Jolley and Publishing Assistant Marsha Luttrell took on the project of a first-time book writer, rendered assistance beyond expectation and brought the volume to life. Their graciousness and professionalism stands behind the MUP imprimatur.

Thank you, everyone.

INDEX